MW00856289

7
CREDIT
LYONNAIS

Book design: Peter Dawson, Namkwan Cho gradedesign.com

3002 Sterling Circle, Suite 100
Boulder, Colorado 80301-2338 USA
E-mail velopress@competitorgroup.com

Distributed in the United States and Canada by Ingram Publisher Services

A Cataloging-in-Publication record for this book is available from the Library of Congress.
ISBN 978-1-937715-68-7

For information on purchasing VeloPress books, please e-mail velopress@competitorgroup.com or visit www.velopress.com.

This paper meets the requirements of ANSI/NISO Z39.48-1992 (Permanence of Paper).

16 17 18 / 10 9 8 7 6 5 4 3 2 1

Published by arrangement with Bluetrain Publishing, London
www.bluetrainpublishing.com

PREVIOUS PAGE

1986 Tour de France: stage 20

Seen from behind in the start house, Greg LeMond waits to begin the last time trial of a Tour that pushed him to the limit, both physically and psychologically.

Greg LeMond
YELLOW JERSEY RACER

GUY ANDREWS

Boulder, Colorado

le coq sportif
TOUR DE FRANCE
L'EQUIPE
CAFE DE COLOMBIA

Contents

1986 Tour de France
Winner of the '86 Tour de France, the first American to take the yellow jersey home.

Foreword

For me, cycling's about more than just the racing. It's a strong part of the culture, but it's not everything. Ever since I first rode a bike, a sense of freedom and escape has been a large part of my life: I've always loved riding my bike. I truly believe that there is no other sport like cycling. It's individual, it's a team sport, it's social, and, although grueling, it's one of the most rewarding sports in the world.

When I was a kid, I wish somebody had been able to tell me, "You're smart, not dumb. You just need a different way of learning." I just couldn't sit still. I got up to all sorts of trouble at school, and was always in the principal's office, telling someone I was sorry. That led to frustration and low self-esteem, but cycling changed all that. Intense physical activity opened my brain to learning. Like most young racers, my cycling education started at a bike shop. It accelerated when I joined the local cycling club, but became ingrained when I met Roland Della Santa. Roland was my first link to the world of professional bicycle racing. He was and still is one of America's best custom bicycle builders. He was also a racer. But most importantly, he was a hoarder of every European cycling magazine there was. Roland had more than fifteen years of French and Italian racing magazines stacked two feet high against the wall of his living room. Of course, I couldn't read them since they were either in French or in Italian, but it didn't matter: it was the photos that told the story.

Eddy Merckx, Felice Gimondi, Luis Ocaña, Roger De Vlaeminck, Freddy Maertens—they all became my heroes. And the Tour of Flanders and Paris-Roubaix became my obsession. The photos of Bernard Thévenet dropping Eddy Merckx, the greatest cyclist of all time, are etched into my memory. The first time I saw the Tour de France in person, in 1978, I knew that cycling was my sport, and that I would be doing everything I could to one day win the Tour myself.

Trying to explain to someone what professional cycling is really like is almost impossible. How do you describe such courses as Paris-Roubaix and the Tour of Flanders, or such events as the Giro d'Italia and the Tour de France? Trying to describe what it feels like to race in these events is even more difficult. But try this for size: take the skills and the sense of speed of a Formula 1 race—although in the American version, Nascar, you can get the drafting effects too—combine these with a marathon and a day at a track and field meet. Do all of these sports on a daily basis for three weeks straight, and you'll begin to get an idea of what bike racing is like. Best of all, though, you're riding through historical villages, climbing and descending some of the world's most beautiful mountains, with more than 15 million fans cheering you on. Well, it doesn't get any better than that!

You could never have an American Tour de France because you could never recreate the history. Think of Wimbledon and tennis, the Masters and golf, Indianapolis and the 500. It's the event, it's the place, and it's the course. In cycling, however, it's even more so. Cycling is historical and classical, but it's about the events. It's the classics, the Monuments, the Grand Tours, the Tour de France. And no matter what, cycling still revolves around "La Grande Boucle." For a bike racer, though, there is much more to it than just the Tour. I loved racing in Belgium, in Italy, and at home in the USA. In all parts of the world, racing a bike is an all-around experience because it changes the way you live, the way you travel, and it allows you to meet some wonderful people along the way.

Guy Andrews was keen for this book to consist of my own thoughts and recollections on my racing career, highlighting some of the key moments that help convey what racing was like during my time in the peloton. And by interviewing some of my friends, teammates, and rivals, it tells the story of my life as a bike racer—of how all of our lives were shaped forever by some great times together and some great races.

When you are racing, you think that cycling revolves around you as a racer. Eventually, when you retire and look back on your career, you realize that it's the events that made the races, not the other way round. Every year, there are new actors in the Tour de France, and every year that race creates a star. But there is always a new star racer—and the racing is always as dramatic.

Greg LeMond

1986 Tour de France: stage 18
After the race to Alpe d'Huez.

Introduction

Greg LeMond planned his cycling career meticulously. When he set out, he wrote a short list of the goals he wanted to achieve. A short list of big objectives. He wanted to win the biggest cycling races, and he was impatient, too. He wanted to do great things—and fast.

But being a three-time Tour de France winner is only half the story of Greg LeMond's racing career. He is the first and only American cyclist to have won the Tour de France, certainly, but Greg wasn't only interested in that three-week race in July. Nowadays, people forget that being a professional cyclist in the 1980s meant a long and tough season: racing flat out from February to October. Greg was one of the all-around riders able to compete over a full racing season, just as much at home on the cobbles of the arduous spring classics as he was on the sun-baked mountains of the summer months' Grand Tours.

The sport of cycling can act like a cocoon for professional cyclists, protecting them from the 'real' world.

As Greg says in his foreword to this book, bike racing is not about the riders, it's about the races themselves and their ability to conjure up a spirit of competition and adventure. In the summer of 1986, a group of friends and I cycled from Leicester in central England to Nantes on the west coast of France to watch that year's Tour. We traveled light and camped every night along the way. Like many British cycling fans of the time, we had no real idea what the Tour was going to be like; we also knew very little about the riders. Obviously, we knew something of the English-speaking riders, but the Belgian, Dutch, German, Italian, French, and Spanish names were all a bit of a mystery—in part because, to us, the sport itself was still a mystery.

Nevertheless, as bike racers have for decades, we rode our bikes religiously every weekend, read everything we could, pored over photographs in the magazines, and watched what little of the Tour we could on TV. Whatever information you're able to gather, though, can never prepare you for the size and excitement that the Tour de France provides. Even in this age of 24/7 Internet and TV sports coverage, as live sporting spectacles go, the Tour is hypnotizing: seeing the riders right there in front of you, recognizing the names and faces you've seen only in magazines. Strangely, however, it's not the racing that stays with you as much as the atmosphere, the color, and the crowds. My lasting memories are of the sounds we heard: the tootling horns, the accordion music, the ever-present voice of the finishing-line announcer, Daniel Mangeas. Even today, I can hear him enthusiastically mispronounce the non-French riders' names, with one name in particular standing out: "Gray-gorry Lee-monde."

I'm sure I'm not the first to say this, but the 1986 Tour de France ignited in me a lifelong passion for bike racing. It was one of the most exciting editions in its history, and Greg's victory was hard-earned, problematic, and tense—which is fitting for an event as arduous as the Tour.

I first met Greg in 2007, for a magazine interview over breakfast at Claridge's hotel in London. He didn't have much time, he said, asking, would it take very long? We met, we ate breakfast—and then sat around chatting for several hours. Bearing in mind the timing of the interview, I had the impression that the LeMonds were under siege from all sides. The threats and legal shenanigans were taking their toll: they were clearly at the end of a very difficult period in their lives. In the end, I couldn't print most of the interview, as it would undoubtedly have caused even more trouble for them. There was too much at stake at the time, and some of what Greg told me even I found hard to believe. There was one thing, however, that Greg was certainly right about: the proverbial shit was about to hit the proverbial fan. In fact, it seems that despite being the "last to know" when doping was going on around him, Greg now has a canny knack of predicting the future—good and bad—of cycling.

The sport of cycling can act like a cocoon for professional riders, protecting them from the "real" world. Although being brought up in an environment that nurtures physical pain and suffering as a way of life clearly defines them, they can often disappear into themselves, becoming quiet and withdrawn. But they can also appear tough and hardened by their sport, and some retire simply to play harder, drifting into drinking, smoking, and sometimes worse. Talking to Greg, however, quickly reminds you that cyclists are only human.

"I raced for fourteen years, and bike riders are nice guys," LeMond says. "It's easy to forget that they are actually just kids, even at twenty-five. Their moral judgment is like that of a teenager. They're so focused

1986 Tour de France: stage 21
At the start of the stage from Saint Étienne to the Puy-de-Dôme.

1986 Tour de France
Greg being interviewed
by CBS television.

on their sport that they're not able to look outside in a mature way. And they are so easily influenced. But they are not bad: very few of these cyclists are cheaters or bad people. I'm sure they just want to keep up and do the sport they love and keep it on a level playing field."

Ex-professionals have a habit of knowing when a race is going to get tough. Most TV commentators miss the subtle signs: a dropped head, the straightening arms, the looking over the shoulder, the resignation in a rider's body language when a break is about to fail or when they realize they've simply run out of road. Greg LeMond talks about racing like any other European ex-pro. When he talks about cycling hard, he pushes his thumb under his chin and pushes it forward, the European sign for "on the hook," what the Italians would call "al gancio," and what the English-speakers call "on the rivet": at full speed. Greg still talks in the language of the peloton, a mixture of French, Italian, and English. The vocabulary is a product of tradition and habit, but more Belgian than Californian.

Being in a 1980s cycling team—even a progressive one like Renault—was a little like joining the army. The workload alone was immense.

This all seems rather unnatural for LeMond, mostly because he spent the majority of his fourteen year professional racing career as an outsider. While the rest of the peloton followed the rules—ate what they were told to eat, wore what they were told to wear, and generally stuck to tradition—Greg stood out. Rules in cycling are everywhere: what to do, what to say, even how to "be." As a result, today's riders seem to have blended into one, their personality and opinions having been hammered out of them. In Greg's mind, however, the rules were there to be broken. "I couldn't take things for granted. I love the tradition of the sport, but I rebelled against it if it didn't make sense to me."

The approach taken to Greg's career by both him and his wife Kathy was fittingly subversive too. They married almost on the eve of traveling to Europe, determined not to be split up by Greg's new career path. From that point on, they often traveled to races and training camps as a couple, and would be together whenever they could for the next fourteen years. This, however, wasn't the way it was done. Cycling was and still is very much a man's world. Although Kathy was as belligerent and stubborn as Greg, creating with her husband an alliance that no directeur sportif could break, it appeared that the more obstacles that were put in their way, the stronger they became. What's more, they had a plan, which, as Kathy recalls, was as matter-of-fact as could be: "We decided to go over there, and Greg would race until he was twenty-three. If he hadn't made a living by then, we'd come home."

Kathy needn't have worried: by the time Greg was twenty-three, he'd won more races than many talented professionals achieve in their whole careers, including the World Championships at the age of twenty-two. Kathy definitely wouldn't be going home just yet. They were going to have to stay.

Greg and Kathy are like any happily married couple: they talk almost as one, sometimes even answering for each other. And as much as they share their frustrations over the difficulties of the past few decades since Greg retired, they also share a detailed understanding of and passion for the sport of cycle racing.

In Greg's era, talented young riders were usually nurtured and bossed around by a team's directeur sportif or one of his assistants, usually ex-racers themselves. Put simply, it was how it had always been done. But what the LeMonds were trying to do certainly wasn't. Cyrille Guimard had signed Greg to be the next protégé for his Renault "superteam." He learned some English and agreed to let Greg travel home a few times a year, relaxed the rules a little, and also accepted that Greg wanted to do things his way.

There's no doubt that Guimard was different. Many now recognize that it was he who introduced the changes that would eventually bring the modern sport of cycling into being: the use of aerodynamics, the special time trial bikes, deep section wheels, and bladed spokes allied with changing opinions on diet, hydration, and training. But his ability to manage big egos was also critical. By putting together a cycling team made up of highly talented individuals who could be rotated as necessary, he had strength in depth and arrived at races with riders who were fit rather than fatigued. It was early days for the concept of marginal gains, but, as ex-pro David Millar said of Guimard, "He was Sky before Sky."

However, being in a 1980s cycling team—even a progressive one like Renault—was still a little like joining the army. The workload alone was immense. Behind the scenes, too, cycling remained in the Dark Ages, and women were most definitely not welcome. Neither were those from beyond the borders of cycling's heartlands. And, as Greg recalls from his Renault days, if you were on a French team, you would have to learn to speak French: "The team were told by Guimard not to speak English with me, only French, so I learned a bit. Then, when we all came to the USA to ride the Red Zinger [later the Coors Classic] in 1981, I took the team for some real Mexican food in Boulder, Colorado. There's some nice looking waitresses, and all of a sudden Marc Madiot and the boys could all speak perfect English! I couldn't believe it! The whole time I'm struggling to keep up with them because they speak so fast. In the first six

1986: Lisieux, post-Tour criterium
When Greg was a kid, he had posters of the Belgian Eddy Merckx on his wall. After his first Tour de France victory, French kids wanted posters of the American Greg LeMond on their walls. Like Merckx, Greg's determination and tenacity were born at an early age, as Greg explained to the journalist Sam Abt after his Tour win in 1986: "I wanted to be a successful cyclist, so when I was seventeen [in 1978], I wrote down what I wanted to achieve on a piece of paper: win the Junior Worlds in 1979, win the Olympic road race in 1980, win the professional World Championships by the time I was twenty-two or twenty-three, and by the time I was twenty-four or twenty-five win the Tour de France." Such ambitions sound fantastic, unbelievable even, and impossible for someone at such a young age to imagine. And yet Greg realized them all (except the Olympics, but 1980 was the year of the US boycott, and put that particular goal out of reach). However, "impossible" was a word rarely used by Greg. In fact, the harder and more unattainable something appeared to be, the more he wanted to do it.

coq sportif
TERSPORT

weeks of being on the road in France, I read loads of books at the dining table because they spoke so quickly. Despite that, and looking back now, I trusted all my teammates on the French teams I rode with. I'd go back any day to a French team. I didn't like France much at first, but I eventually learned the language and I learned to love the French."

In bike racing, there have been many careers that have withered even before they've had a chance to blossom: if you didn't have the talent, you'd be on the first train home soon enough. A few non-European riders had made it as professionals before Greg, but few had his talent or his tenacity. For every cycling star, there are a dozen more with similar attributes, similar engines, similar equipment, support, and enthusiasm. But tenacity?

Greg talks quickly, and usually with a smile. He jokes about the fact that he was shot twice, the first time by his friend, rival, and teammate Bernard Hinault during a trip to his father's ranch in Nevada . . . He also makes light of his achievements, but beneath this breezy exterior is a competitor's spirit and a strong sense of fair play and loyalty.

Greg is arguably one of the last generation of 'gentleman racers,' someone who rode on his own strengths rather than exploiting others' weaknesses.

Somewhat ironically, Greg LeMond is perhaps the worst timekeeper I have ever met—myself included. You'll get the stories if you can get him in front of you, but that in itself is an operation that requires much patience and planning. And when you do get to see him, it's fast, in all senses of the word. The journalist and writer Matt Seaton, a man who is rarely ruffled, had told me as much before I traveled to Minneapolis to meet Mr. LeMond. "Never get in a car he's driving," he warned. "Seriously. He really does think he's Stirling Moss. Only faster, and with a sadistic streak."

Just before starting work on Greg's story, I was in Paris carrying out research for a different book. Greg and Kathy happened to be there too—as guests at the French Open tennis tournament at Roland-Garros—so we met for coffee. Greg arrived for our meeting on a Velib, a Paris city bike, an hour late and sweating profusely. He then apologized just as profusely and disappeared to take a shower and get ready for his next meeting—which he was already late for. And in all the interviews I've done about Greg, each and every one of the interviewees has smiled, shrugged, and said, "That's Greg." Kathy once told me that she thinks Greg is shy, that he doesn't want to be the center of attention. But he attracts attention by his very nature.

Alex Jacome, the son of Greg's longtime soigneur Otto Jacome, went to races with Greg when they were young. He too picked up on Greg's star appeal and warm, generous personality: "He's probably a greater human being off the bike . . . but I've never met someone that attracts people like Greg does."

Greg's life has certainly seen its fair share of turmoil and heartbreak, not only before he started racing, but also while he was racing and after he'd retired. However, this book isn't about what happened before or after Greg's career; rather, this book is a pure celebration of his ability and talents as the best American bike racer in history. That's why, in the pages that follow, his story is told through his friends, his rivals, and his teammates—those who knew him best, and those who knew him as a bike racer. In all these interviews, what comes across most clearly is the nature of Greg's race craft. He is arguably one of the last of the "gentlemen racers," someone who rode on his own strengths rather than exploiting others' weaknesses. To him, however, that's just the way it was done. "All I needed was to know who was good at the time. I had no grudge against anyone when I was racing, and I didn't compete with any animosity or anger."

These days, Greg LeMond is genial, friendly, and troubled by relatively little. His no-nonsense reaction to the traditions of European bike racing was revolutionary. The previously conservative and introspective mentality of bike racing in the 1980s needed shaking up, from top to bottom. Greg wasn't just a great bike racer, he was also a catalyst for change in professional cycling, spearheading the modern era. In the 1980s and 1990s, bike racers, once known as "Les Forçats de la Route" (The Convicts of the Road), took charge of their own affairs—mostly because of Greg. He saw to it that the salaries of professional cyclists were raised dramatically, and, more importantly, how their contracts were negotiated.

Greg's ideas on diet, training, and monitoring performance were truly innovative. To this day, young riders still emulate many of the ideas and approaches he introduced to cycling. He also ensured that product endorsement benefited not only the team but also the individual rider. And he injected some much-needed fun and color into the sport too, bringing in American-style sports marketing and commercial innovation. There have, of course, been many riders who have won more races and had longer careers, but most of them have had little or no influence on the sport of cycling in general. His legacy goes far beyond being a yellow jersey racer, because, in the history of the sport, few riders have changed it as much or as creatively as Greg LeMond has. He has left an indelible mark.

Guy Andrews

"My dad bought a bike and we just started riding together. He wanted to lose some weight; he was going through a bit of a midlife crisis, and probably wanted to reconnect with his family. We rode together all the way through the winter. I was trying to get in shape for skiing. My first ride was in August of 1975 in Carson City, Nevada, but I was pretty wiped out. The first time racing, I didn't know what I was doing. We did three or four laps, but no one told me what to do—the most I had done [up to that point] was race with my dad."

Greg LeMond

"Thinking back to when we were teenagers, we'd always talked about making a living being bike racers, but it was just a dream. To have it happen and come to fruition . . . it was a special time for sure."

JEFF BRADLEY

PREVIOUS SPREAD
Summer of 1980
Greg racing in France.

ABOVE
1978 US National Junior Road Race Championships, Milwaukee, WI
During their early racing careers, Jeff Bradley (pictured here) and Greg would trade numerous national titles.

American Flyers

In 1978, Jeff Bradley was one of a new breed of American cyclists, capturing the imagination of US cycling fans when he, Ron Kiefel, Greg Demgen, and Greg LeMond won a bronze medal in the team time trial at the Junior World Championships in Washington, DC. It doesn't sound like much now, but along with Connie Carpenter's silver medal in the women's road race at the 1977 World Championships, this was one of the first USA cycling medals since 1969, when Audrey McElmury had won a surprise gold at the Worlds. Small change for many European nations, but this was the start of a renaissance for US cycling.

At the end of the 1970s, cycling was an also-ran sport in the United States; even such winter sports as skiing and speed skating were more popular. However, with the benefits of crossover fitness training beginning to influence the world of winter sports, the summer pursuit of cycling proved ideal for the winter sports' off-season. Such athletes as Carpenter and Eric Heiden, both of whom had competed at the Winter Olympics as speed skaters, were now looking to cycling for a fresh challenge. As a skier, Greg too had found his way into cycling via a winter sport, as had his friend and arch-rival Jeff Bradley, another former speed skater. Having made the summer switch to two wheels, neither Jeff nor Greg ever looked back.

In 1979, Jeff finished fourth in the Junior World Championships in Argentina, beating a soon-to-be classics ace, the Belgian Eric Vanderaerden, in the bunch sprint; Greg had already won the race from a three-man breakaway. Also in Argentina, Jeff and Greg won another bronze medal in the team time trial—to match the one they had netted the year before—but this time with Andy Hampsten and Mark Fris. A renowned sprinter, Jeff chalked up around 150 wins in his career, racing all over the United States and Europe, and reaching a high with a ride in the 1987 Tour de France with the 7-Eleven team, his first and last attempt at the Tour. Today, Jeff runs a bike shop in Davenport, Iowa.

It's hard not to find similarities between the fictional racers in the films *Breaking Away* (1979) and *American Flyers* (1985) and the lives of Jeff, Greg, and the rest of the late-1970s American cycling fraternity. Without doubt, the photographs of the early races in which Jeff and his peers competed immediately bring to mind the "Cutters" team in *Breaking Away*, in which a group of young racers takes on the might of an Italian cycling squad (in the case of the Cold War–themed *American Flyers*, the out-of-town competitors are bearded Soviets). Despite the filmmakers' naive misunderstanding of the sport of cycling, the parallels between fact and fiction remain: the camaraderie among the racers, the coming-of-age stories, and the road trips of many thousands of miles to compete in races across the United States will all ring true with many American riders of the time.

1977–80:
Jeff Bradley

"I first met Greg when we were probably fourteen or fifteen years old. It was on the track at Northbrook, just outside of Chicago. We'd heard of each other: stories went back and forth for quite some time, and Greg was the 'sensation' coming out of the West Coast. We were both young kids, and the sport was much smaller at that time, so everybody could easily keep track of everybody else throughout the country. We were still in the Intermediate category at that point—we were not yet in Juniors—and it was the National Championships. We hit it off as friends right from the start. We battled a lot head-to-head as youngsters, but we were always friends and rivals. We were never at war with each other.

"Like Eric Heiden, Connie Carpenter, and others, I had crossed over to cycling from speed skating. Back in the mid- to late '70s and '80s, a lot of the speed skaters raced bikes in the summertime. Especially in the Midwest, there were families who messed around with bicycle racing. For me, I was just a much better cyclist than speed skater, and I enjoyed it a lot more too. It was much more interesting. You start out, you can travel with the family to local races, and as your success comes you get more offers from sponsors and you make it to the national team and things blossom from there. We had a great time. I was much better at the sport as an amateur when it was fun, when it wasn't all business. That's the way we started out in the US.

"Greg was a fly-by-the-seat-of-your-pants kind a guy, and he needed the guidance back then. We would go out and party a little too much."

"Greg and I became close friends when we entered the Juniors category. In those days, it covered three age groups: sixteen-, seventeen-, and eighteen-year-olds. The first time we spun out together was the Junior Worlds trials in Princeton, New Jersey, where the age bracket was seventeen- and eighteen-year-olds; we were still sixteen and so too young to qualify. When we were racing together during that time, it often came down to being between Greg and me. Anyway, Greg placed first and second in the Junior Worlds trials. He was easily the best. It was an eye-opener: the guy just had an extra gear, something way beyond special. It was 1977 when he won the Nationals; after that we traded off National Championships back and forth [over] the three years we were Juniors, and then he won the Junior Worlds in Argentina when we were eighteen-year-olds.

"America had been in the doldrums [in terms of bike racing], and then all of a sudden we started to put in performances at world and Olympic level. I think it was more than just raw talent. Obviously, Greg had bucket-loads of talent, but there was a spirit among us too. At the Junior Worlds in Argentina in 1979, the team was Greg, Andy Hampsten, Mark Fris, and myself, and we really thought we could win that race [they eventually came third]. We had a lot of morale . . . especially for 'outsiders'! That really carried through to the following year. We were no longer Juniors, and were competing with much older and more experienced guys, but we were absolutely as good or better than our seniors, who were five to ten years older than us.

"I remember those first European amateur races: the Ruban Granitier Breton, Circuit de la Sarthe, and Circuit des Ardennes. All the national teams would be there and we held our own. Americans had never held their own in the past, and we were winning these races. Greg won the Circuit de la Sarthe [in 1980], with guys like Cyrille Guimard saying, 'Who's this American kid stomping on all the Russians and East Germans?' But as kids, we all did pretty well too. It wasn't really just Greg; we were all in there.

"In the team time-trial situations, Greg was always the strongest guy. In particular, at the Junior Worlds in Argentina, Hampsten crashed out halfway through; our other teammate, Mark Fris, was sitting at the back so we had to keep slowing down to keep from dropping him; and Greg was doing 80 percent of the work. Well, if we'd had another contributor, if Andy hadn't crashed, or we hadn't had to slow down to keep our third guy on . . . OK, so maybe we wouldn't have won, but who knows what could have happened?

"Eddie B. [Eddie Borysewicz, the legendary Polish-born American national coach at the time] paid very close attention to the team time trial. He was an awesome coach, and had a lot to do with nurturing Greg's early years. If anybody called the shots, it would have been Eddie B. He kept a tight rein on Greg; he focused in and helped him find his way. He would have pushed himself too hard in a training situation otherwise, because even as a sixteen-, seventeen-year-old, Greg could take a high volume of training. So, on his own: he was a fly-by-the-seat-of-your-pants kind a guy, and he needed the guidance back then. We would go out and party a little too much. We had to be reined in a few times; we had to slow down. We definitely didn't do everything right, but it was good to have the US Cycling Federation coaching staff with us. They did a great job for the time. They did well, but the whole successes of the late '70s was down to talent, enthusiasm, good team morale, and Eddie B.

"Of course, the team time trial was quite an intense event for Juniors—seventy-five kilometers, with nowhere to hide—but we were good at it and we trained specifically for that event. It was the one event that was less of a lottery, so less work was involved. Eddie B. had a lot of experience with team time trials, and that was the one thing he was going for which guaranteed success, so that's what we were focused on. During that period, Greg and I spent a lot of time together at the Olympic training centers. That was our first experience of training camp with the coaches for two weeks. We spent a bit of time at the Colorado Springs Olympic training center too. We were super-serious: for us, it was our leaving-high-school-and-going-to-college era.

"We did a lot of training for the team time trial. A lot. Much of it was spent behind a motorbike, narrowing down the longlist [of potential team members] throughout the season. We'd start with six, or eight, or ten guys and the list would just get narrower and narrower until we found what worked.

1984 Coors Classic
Jeff Bradley climbs with Canadian Steve Bauer on the Morgul-Bismark stage.

1978 US National Junior Road Race Championships, Milwaukee, WI
From left: Greg Demgen (4th), Greg LeMond (2nd), Jeff Bradley (1st), Steve Wood (3rd), and Ron Kiefel (5th). Together, these riders would form the basis of US success at the Junior World Championships in 1978 and 1979.

That continued, even after Greg left and turned pro. It continued all the way through the '84 Olympics with Eddie B. and the time-trial squad: Ron Kiefel, Davis Phinney, Thurlow Rogers, Roy Knickman, Andy Weaver, and myself. We were all kind of in the mix of that group all the way through '83, '84.

"Greg could take the beatings much better than the average guy. He had so much natural raw talent, he could survive all the hard races and the sicknesses and bounce back from them."

"As amateurs, we would go over and do those small-stage spring races in France. Greg was already riding for Renault and living in Nantes, but we would get together. I would go stay with Greg for three, four, five days at a time, and the US team . . . we'd have a spell of not racing where I'd go hang out with Greg. So I did actually see him a bit. Back then, there was no Internet, and even a telephone call back to the States was awful expensive, so it was like isolation. Greg had a nice house to live in, but there was no English-speaking anything. The lifestyle, the food, the weather—everything was different. And the racing turned into much more difficult racing.

"Right after the Olympics in '84, that's when all the talk of a US pro team started, mainly Jim Ochowicz [the future team's manager and current team boss at BMC] and the 7-Eleven crowd, making the decision to take a load of us from the amateur ranks and see if we could compete as professionals. By the mid-'80s, Greg had already broken the ice; he was already a force to be reckoned with as a pro. That's how the whole thing started. At the beginning of '85, around late February/early March, I started as a pro for 7-Eleven, and we went over [to Europe] for the Giro d'Italia and Tour de France.

"Greg had changed a lot by the time we started taking part in the pro races, even physiologically. He was way more cut out for it, and could take the beatings much better than the average guy. He had so much natural raw talent, he could survive all the hard races and the sicknesses and bounce back from them. He was the cream that came to the top and was obviously special. [At 7-Eleven] we were all doing the same thing; we didn't have any standout guys. As we got more experience, we managed to scratch out some results here and there—guys like Ron Kiefel and Davis Phinney, and then later Andy Hampsten—but it took a while. With Greg, however, you could tell it was coming. He was in there fighting. Thinking back to when we were fifteen-, sixteen-, seventeen-year-olds, we'd always talked about making a living being bike racers, but it was just a dream. To have it happen and come to fruition . . . it was a special time for sure. It was a lot of fun, but especially for Greg. Holy cow! He was a warrior and had a head for the game. And he had it all written down: he had his goals in front of him all that time.

"Greg maintained a façade, too, that he was always a bit of a joker. He'd go out drinking, and we'd be normal American kids having a great time, but then Greg was just a winner. He would never back down, and I think he thrived on pressure. Even going way back to our early years, the more the odds were stacked against him, the more determined he'd be to overcome them. At the Junior Worlds in Argentina, he got hooked under the tires by Kenny De Maerteleire and actually crossed the line second [Greg was forced into the curb by the Belgian, and had to jump a row of tires. He broke a couple of spokes in his rear wheel but still came back to finish second. De Maerteleire was later penalized for his actions, and the positions were reversed]. That would have knocked most people out of the race, but Greg wouldn't give in. I think that's the one quality of his that really stands out: he would never back down. Ever."

77

Team: amateur junior

1st: US National Junior Road Race Championships

Team: US national team and amateur junior

2nd: US National Junior Road Race Championships

9th: UCI Junior Road World Championships (Washington, DC)
3rd: team time trial (with Jeff Bradley, Greg Demgen, and Ron Kiefel)

Team: US national team and amateur junior

1st: UCI Junior Road World Championships (Buenos Aires, Argentina)
2nd: pursuit
3rd: team time trial (with Mark Fris, Jeff Bradley, and Andy Hampsten)

1st: US National Junior Road Race Championships

4th: Red Zinger Classic (open)

Team: Lejeune (amateur)

1st: Circuit de la Sarthe
2nd: stage 4a
5th: stage 3

1st: Lima Road Race (Colombia)

3rd: Circuit des Ardennes
1st: stage 5

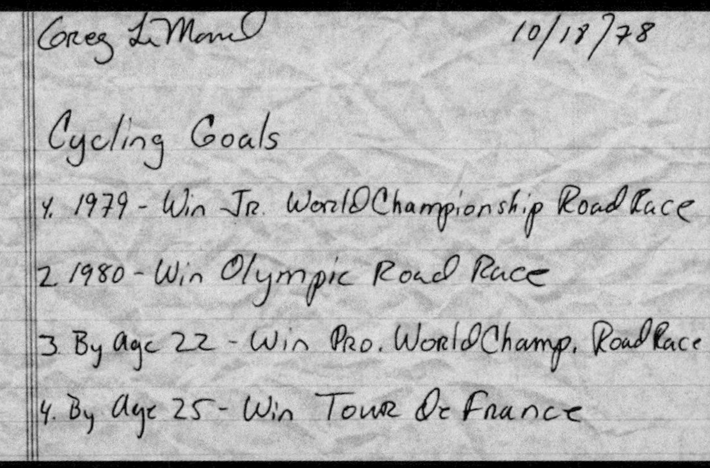

Greg LeMond 10/18/78

Cycling Goals

1. 1979 - Win Jr. World Championship Road Race
2. 1980 - Win Olympic Road Race
3. By age 22 - Win Pro. World Champ. Road Race
4. By age 25 - Win Tour De France

“I wanted something more challenging than going up a ski lift and whizzing back down. I was interested in sports where I could accomplish something myself without having to depend on others. There were friends around, but when you live in the countryside, your closest friends are miles away.”

Greg LeMond

"I always wanted to keep moving and improving."

Greg LeMond

"When I got into cycling, I bought a Raleigh Grand Prix. It was red and black. I stumbled into cycling through riding with my dad. I didn't know anything—I happened to ride through the winter in Reno, and I ran into a guy [Cliff Young] at Rick's Bike Shop in January '76. He seemed to be recruiting bike riders to get into racing. He asked me if I had any interest in racing, and I said I didn't. He said, 'Well, come to a meeting in two weeks' time and see if you're interested.' [The meeting] was like hearing people talk a foreign language, but two weeks later my dad and I showed up at a race. I was in tennis shoes, running shorts, and a tank top; everyone else was on their Italian bikes. Anyways, I ended up getting second place. We had a national champion in the group and some very experienced racers who couldn't believe I got second place, and they were saying to my dad, 'Your son has got a lot of talent.'"

Greg LeMond

ABOVE, TOP **Greg and Kathy** An early demonstration of Greg's bike handling skills.

"In those first five years—God, it was fun. It's hard to explain how [my early years in cycling] were so dynamic for me, because I went from not even thinking about racing to winning. Up until turning pro, it was the most fun I had in my career. I did my first race in a tank top and tennis shoes on a Raleigh Grand Prix, and I won the first eleven races I [competed in]. Once or twice a week I went to Roland Della Santa's shop [in Reno] just to hang out while he worked. He'd tell me stories about the great European stars, the thousands of screaming fans, and legendary races like the Tour de France and Giro d'Italia. In the summer of 1978, I won two races in Switzerland, two in France, and six out of eight races in Belgium. Noël Dejonckheere was a Belgian pro who came over to the USA during the Tour de France in '76, and I just met him and he rode with me even though I had been racing only for four or five months. He went back and told his parents he had seen the next Eddy Merckx! So that had already been spread around by the time I got to Belgium in 1978."

Greg LeMond

"In the summer of '78, we did a ride from Geneva to the Col de Joux Plane, near Morzine in the Alps. A group of us from Geneva Cycling Club, we watched the Tour de France go over the mountain from the chalet belonging to Jean-Claude Killy [a French alpine ski racer and fellow member of the Geneva CC]. When I saw the race, I knew that was what I wanted to do."

Greg LeMond

ABOVE

1980 Circuit de la Sarthe

The first "big" win of Greg's career. The Circuit de la Sarthe is a short, early season stage race held in the Loire region of France. It's usually contested by newly professional riders, with some amateur and national teams mixed in.

ABOVE, RIGHT

1980 Circuit de la Sarthe

"There was this attitude that Europe was mythical and that we American cyclists could never compete. Obviously, I didn't buy into that. Eddy Merckx and those guys—they all put their pants on the same way I did, so why wouldn't I be able to go out there and win?"

Greg LeMond

"For a cyclist, the Olympics are just a stepping stone. The Tour de France is where the best competition is: it's what cycling is all about. So in 1980, when the US team boycotted the Olympics in Moscow, I turned pro."

Greg LeMond

"When I first went to Europe, in 1981, I signed as a professional for 6,000 French francs [around $15,000]. But in 1980, I had been making $30,000 racing as an amateur in the US, so it was a sizable pay cut. I thought it was worth it, though, because Renault was a great team and [Cyrille] Guimard was such a good coach."

Greg LeMond

RENAULT
SR
Coors
elf
GITANE

"So we get to the first race, very early in the morning, a very motley group. In the middle of it is a goofy-looking kid with a canary-yellow jersey and a canary-yellow bike and this bushy hair and this funny-looking helmet. He looked ridiculous, pitiful."

KENT GORDIS

PREVIOUS SPREAD

Coors Classic

Greg won the 1981 Coors Classic by more than five minutes, beating all the home teams and a powerful Soviet squad. The race became an inspiration for the film *American Flyers*, written by Steve Tesich (who had also written the script for *Breaking Away*).

ABOVE

Kent Gordis in 1977.

A Most Excellent Adventure

Kent Gordis, the renowned American television producer, was born in New York City in 1961. His father was a New York native, his mother a Russian émigré who had come to the United States after the Second World War. When Kent was only eighteen months old, his father landed a job as a computer programmer for a financial institution in Switzerland. Kent's formative years were therefore spent in Geneva, surrounded by mountains. When Kent turned twelve, he and his younger brother returned to the United States and eventually settled in Berkeley, California, where Kent would spend his teenage years—and where he started racing bikes.

Kent proved to be a successful junior racer. Unlike Greg, however, he decided to hang up his wheels early on, swapping them for textbooks and heading off to study at Yale University. His childhood in Europe had fueled an enthusiasm for bike racing, however, and his ability to speak French put him in good stead for his later career as a TV producer on the Tour de France and other major cycling events. The coverage of the Seoul and Barcelona Olympics he co-produced for NBC won him two Emmys.

In the late 1980s, Kent teamed up with Greg to write *Greg LeMond's Complete Book of Cycling* (1987). Despite the training techniques it outlines being a little dated, the book still has much to say about being a bike racer: the physiology is still current, and the racing knowledge—the tips about tactics and technique—is astute and well informed. Perhaps the book is founded on the experiences and enthusiasm that its authors began to acquire as young American racers, from reading *Miroir du cyclisme*, and from dreaming of the Tour de France.

Without Kent and his family, Greg may not have gone to Europe when he did. Once there, however, he embarked on a remarkable journey from unknown schoolboy racer to the next Tour de France prodigy.

1981:
Kent Gordis

"I'm one day older than Greg. When we were fourteen, I was nostalgic for my time in Europe; cycling was a very European-identified sport back then. The first race I competed in was in March 1976. Before that, I had been training with Velo Club Berkeley, which was one of the big clubs in America. In the club, we had a guy called George Mount; he was an adult, I was a kid. Later that year, he finished sixth in the Olympics in Montreal. I was able to keep up with Mount [during training], so I thought, when we get to the actual races, I'm gonna clean up. So we get to the first race, very early in the morning, a very motley group. In the middle of it is a goofy-looking kid with a canary-yellow jersey and a canary-yellow bike and this bushy hair and this funny-looking helmet. He looked ridiculous, pitiful. So the race takes off and this pitiful-looking kid breaks away, really strong. I tried to stay with him but it was hard. At the end, he beat me. I was devastated: having stayed [on the same level as] Mount, I couldn't believe it. This small kid was Greg, and we became

"The only race I lost back then was to Kent Gordis, because it was a five kilometer race of ten laps. He got a fifty meter gap from the first corner. Kent was the one who really filled me in on why I shouldn't be wearing yellow jerseys—I raced in it because it matched my bike. This guy ended up attacking me with real attitude; he probably didn't like me because I turned up in this yellow jersey! But that's how we became friends."

Greg LeMond

friends from that day on. That race was twenty-four miles long, which was appropriate for our age category, but the third-placed rider was over ten minutes behind! Greg was from northern Nevada, which was combined with northern California as one racing district. Every weekend we could have competed against each other.

"It's bizarre, strange: any winner has to be tough. In cycling, there's so much pain and dedication, it seems almost contradictory. Extreme winning is almost a pathology . . ."

"In those days, we were so isolated. European cycling had a mythological quality to us on the West Coast. I remember going to a French bookstore in San Francisco where we would get this French magazine about cycling, *Miroir du cyclisme*. It cost fourteen dollars, and I would translate for Greg. It was like an episode from a cartoon: 'Oh look! Eddy Merckx!' We were so taken by the heroism and the grandiosity. Greg knew that if he had to prove himself, he had to go to Europe. My father still lived in Switzerland, and I would spend every summer with him. In the summer of 1979, Greg came along.

"Everyone warned Greg about culture shock, which to me didn't apply. But a lot of Americans felt very out of place: the culture was very different, and again, this was at a time when American culture was more innocent or naive. There was no connection. So Greg stepped off the plane—and just didn't feel any culture shock! Greg was very open-minded, and he always had a structure. Older riders were dogged learners [but Greg wasn't].

"Greg would stay with my family and we would each have eighteen yogurts for dessert! We lived in Geneva, right next to the French border, but I had never raced in Switzerland. Cycling was a very French sport in those days. I was part of a club in Annecy, and Greg came and joined it and started winning right off the bat; clearly, something really important was happening. In that first season, I was Greg's biggest rival. But every year, he developed dramatically and I didn't. Greg was on a higher plane, and below him was about a dozen amateurs. I only raced for about three years. There were other contemporaries of Greg who were far better than me too, people like Andy Hampsten, Davis Phinney . . . all these people were really great, but I was not.

"One of the oddities about Greg is that he was never in with a group. All the other American champions from that generation—Jim Ochowicz, Eric Heiden, and the 7-Eleven crowd—were all part of a group. Ochowicz attempted more than once to get Greg into his team, but Greg always said no. The reasons weren't personal: when he first started, there was no Team 7-Eleven.

"During that first trip [to Geneva], we hopped into my father's car, a 1978 Buick LeSabre station wagon with New Jersey plates—he didn't want to pay the Swiss taxes—and we raced all over Europe. We went to Belgium, Paris, and Greg was winning races, really making a big splash. After that, he became involved in big amateur Paris clubs like Lejeune, and that's how Cyrille Guimard became aware of him. The next year, Cyrille and Bernard Hinault went to Greg's home in Nevada, I was there because I was helping translate. We went to New York for some event, and we were riding along in Central Park when some New York guy recognized Hinault and literally thousands of riders ended up congregating [around him].

"Greg knew that Guimard had been Hinault's coach and had these methods that he admired, and which he still follows today. Greg is really brilliant. He's so brilliant that the physics of his mouth can't keep up with his mind! He moves on to the next point really quickly . . . In terms of training, Greg was Guimard's best student. Greg really started to learn about how the body works. He also knew he needed a strong team to win the Tour de France, and he was never convinced an American team had either the capacity or the technical knowledge to do so. That's why he was never part of the American program. In that sense, there is a similarity between Greg and Lance Armstrong: they were both outsiders. Greg needed to be the outsider; that's what motivated him. We were considered novelties, ridiculous for coming to European cycling in the 1980s. And when Greg didn't join the group, he was also ostracized. He fed off a combination of animosity and isolation. It's bizarre, strange: any winner has to be tough. In cycling, there's so much pain and dedication, it seems almost contradictory. Extreme winning is almost a pathology . . .

"We liked Greg; we admired him. But more than that, he was a family friend. Our main motivation was that he was our friend and to see him succeed was wonderful. When I came back to the US, I had a difficult experience: we essentially moved into what was a heroin hotel. My brother was six years old, and I didn't go to school for a whole year; we were street urchins. But when you're twelve years old, it's not romantic, it's awful. I had this nostalgia for my life in Europe and a mythologized view of Europe and cycling. And I believe I communicated a fair amount of that to Greg. When Greg got to Europe, he was very open about living there and benefiting from the

European lifestyle. A big part of what motivated us was this sense of adventure. The early racing tours we did . . . There's a French expression—*bon enfant*—which means this traditional, French village festival atmosphere. And that's basically what the Tour was in those days. Now it's big business.

"Most big superstars are like brands or products—Beckham, Tiger Woods—and they construct a narrative and manage that narrative, that brand, that value. Greg did none of that . . . he was just a regular guy."

"The first really major victory in Greg's career was the Junior World Championships in Argentina in 1978. And my first reaction was: I'm not so angry any more that he beat me. Over all the years I've known him, the greatest issue that Greg and I had as friends—or as people—was Lance Armstrong. I produced and directed hundreds of races in the Lance period. No matter what my own feelings were, I don't fault people for believing Lance, when Lance and his group of criminal predators took over the sport and sucked the soul out of it. We'd got into cycling for the adventure and the romance, but it was all swept away with this turpentine approach of the Armstrong group, ruining Greg's career and mine: it was because of Lance. The appeal of cycling is the heroism. Most big superstars are like brands or products—Beckham, Tiger Woods—and they construct a narrative and manage that narrative, that brand, that value. Greg did none of that. His agent was his father and he was just a regular guy. In the end, Greg was always genuine and true to himself. Especially in cycling, as we try to recuperate from fifteen years of these criminal predators, it's so refreshing to have [someone like Greg].

"I went to Greg and Kathy's wedding, which was in Kathy's hometown of La Crosse, Wisconsin. I took a plane from NYC to Chicago, changed planes for Chicago to La Crosse—and the airline lost my bag. So I was in my jeans and tatty sneakers, and ended up borrowing a uniform from the hotel bellhop. All I remember is walking into the room and everyone looking around at me and laughing! At that point, I wasn't racing anymore, but Greg was still basically my friend; I was never really directly competitive with him. Straight after the wedding he and Kathy left for Europe. I followed him in the media, which wasn't that easy, and once in a while I'd see him doing well . . . I wouldn't hear from him for nine months or so, and all of a sudden he'd call me and we'd talk until five in the morning and he'd call me for the next two weeks.

"Greg was kind of a hippie. He and I went to a race near Santa Cruz and I actually beat him. It was a quarter-mile too short [for Greg]—he wasn't ready for the finish. So we were coming back from the race and I got an ice cream cone and Greg looked at me with this ice cream cone and was devastated: 'You're eating sugar!' But [his attitude] wasn't a way to get rich, it was a way to get healthy, and he really believed in it; he had principles. A lot of it was down to the way we grew up. The mid-1980s was such a sea change—Adam Smith, the free market—where you could do whatever you could get away with. Look at the Lance scandal. Educated people can't really understand what the problem is.

"Very few people in America have any idea who Greg LeMond is, and he's now the only American who has won the Tour de France. Even when Lance was a brand, nobody was really interested in cycling. During Greg's era, the record TV rating was the final day of the 1989 Tour de France. And that was 5.6 million viewers, which is more than five times the number of people who watched Lance. That's because in those days, cycling wasn't on cable television, it was on network TV—ABC, to be exact. They had it on an anthology show, which had snippets from various sports and then a boxing match: *ABC's Wide World of Sports*. The whole premise of the show was a lot of people waiting to watch boxing . . . Yet that system allowed a lot more people to be brought into cycling.

"In 1986, when Greg won the Tour de France, he was completely spent, (a) because he had just won the Tour, and (b) because of the fight with Hinault. There was a hollowed-out quality to him. I was concerned about my friend; it troubled me a little bit that he was having a hard time. The funny thing about the 1986 Tour—really, the turning point—was Hinault's breakaway in the Pyrenees. Which was stupid: it's where he lost the Tour. If Greg had listened to [La Vie Claire team coach Paul] Koechli and not attacked Hinault, he would not have won the Tour.

"Then, in 1987, I was working at ABC as a production assistant, doing ninety hour weeks. As far as my relationship with Greg was concerned, I just wanted to give him the space to deal with [the shooting] on his own. Which goes back to his position within the group as an outsider: he needed that chip on his shoulder to disprove the negative point of view of the Europeans and the other cyclists [about American riders]. And the shooting was huge. He was completely written off. That was one of the greatest motivators for him: even though he had been close to death, the shooting was a big factor in allowing him to win two more Tours.

"In this era of gross larceny and self-interest, to have somebody like [Greg] who is a prominent person is unbelievably wonderful."

"In 1991, Greg was in the best shape of his life, but all of a sudden he couldn't keep up. The most interesting thing is, Greg had no idea why. Then, in 1999, Greg's watching Lance and is mesmerized—literally watching this unbelievable ride. He's with Julian de Vries, his old Belgian bike mechanic buddy, and Julian says, 'He's on the juice,' and Greg says, 'What do you mean?' He had no idea. That's an amazing declaration of nobility. Here's a guy who, at heart, is a good person. At the end of the day, that's a really wonderful, powerful declaration or description of what Greg LeMond is like, and the period when Greg's principles really shone through was during the Lance years. There was no material gain, and he's gone out of his way not to seek any kind of redemption or material benefit. In this era of gross larceny and self-interest, to have somebody like that who is a prominent figure is unbelievably wonderful."

Summer of 1979
Greg making a name for himself in Belgium, where he won several Junior races.

Team: Renault-Elf-Gitane

1st: Coors Classic
1st: stages 1 and 7

3rd: Critérium du Dauphiné Libéré
5th: stages 5 and 7

3rd: Tour du Tarn
5th: stage 3

5th: Trophée des Grimpeurs

7th: Circuit de la Sarthe

9th: Tour de l'Oise
1st: stage 2
2nd: points classification

11th: Critérium International

18th: Grand Prix de Mauléons-Moulins

47th: UCI Road World Championships (Prague, Czechoslovakia)

54th: Tour of Corsica

112th: Gent-Wevelgem

The 1981 US national cycling team.

"Cyrille Guimard [center, with Bernard Hinault to his left] was probably the finest coach in cycling. He was great at picking young riders and developing them. He was a great psychological support, even coming to my house in Nevada to see how I lived, to understand my background. He understood that I was American, and halfway through the season I would be homesick, and the first couple of years he let me go home, which was a real mental break for me. I liked him."

Greg LeMond

LEFT, TOP Training . . . "When I turned pro [in 1981], I wasn't in the best shape. I had never raced out of shape at that point, and it meant I raced more cautiously. Had I showed up like I was the year before, the racing would not have been so hard. It takes your confidence away; you start to think, what if I'm not as good as I thought I was?"
Greg LeMond

LEFT "I really liked Hinault. He came to my house [in 1981] and treated everyone very well."
Greg LeMond

"My personality was different when I turned pro. Before that, I was so confident and so driven. Joining Renault sounded like a good thing, but it was intimidating because I was always going to be Hinault's domestique. It wasn't that way before I turned pro. It set me back; I started racing more as a teammate, a team rider . . . I was always hesitating."

Greg LeMond

Paris-Roubaix
Yvon Bertin hitches a ride on the press car during a route reconnaissance before the race. In 1981, Paris-Roubaix was won by Bernard Hinault, despite the Frenchman crashing late on. Hinault [pictured center, in the rainbow jersey] always said that he hated the event, regarding it as nonsense; to him, enjoying a race came second to winning it. Greg, on the other hand, appeared to enjoy Paris-Roubaix, relishing the ride across the 'stones.

Paris–Roubaix
"I raced at Paris–Roubaix every year—except for '82, when I'd broken my collarbone. It was my favorite race. The first time I rode it I was nineteen. I did pretty well: I was with Hinault and made it to about 220 or 230 kilometers."
Greg LeMond

Paris–Roubaix
“I was getting tired and Hinault asked me to attack one final time. It was just leading up to some cobblestones, and I did one last massive attack and strung out the field for the next cobblestones sector. Hinault counterattacked, and that was when he broke away to win. I quit right after that—I was just cooked.”
Greg LeMond

Critérium du Dauphiné Libéré
"I was a nineteen-year-old kid far away from home. So Guimard took English lessons so he could talk to me; he made a huge effort. He would ask all the time, 'How are you doing?' and 'What were you doing today?'"
Greg LeMond

"We were treated so well in Belgium, and still are: it's a part of their culture there. Sure, it's a big sport in France, but in Belgium, and especially West Flanders, they just live and breathe the sport of cycling."

PHIL ANDERSON

PREVIOUS SPREAD

Tour de l'Avenir

Signing on at the "Tour of the Future," the week-long stage race regarded as the Tour de France for new professionals and amateurs.

ABOVE

1981 Tour de France: stage 16

Phil Anderson wearing the white jersey as leading young rider at the Tour de France. He had earlier won stage 2, and would wear the yellow jersey for a total of nine stages. Here, he climbs his way towards Morzine.

Flying by the Seat of his Pants

Like all the English-speaking riders in the early 1980s, Phil Anderson was something of a novelty. Perhaps especially so, as Australian cyclists didn't travel much back then, and even fewer had competed in the Tour de France. Anderson, however, was certainly no joke when it came to bike racing. In 1981, he became the first non-European to wear the yellow jersey at the Tour de France; and in 1982, he wore the jersey for no fewer than nine days, undoubtedly influencing a generation of Australian cyclists in the process, and establishing himself as a star of the future. He and Greg met early on in their racing careers, and although they were on rival teams, the two men became training partners and friends, living close to each other in West Flanders, Belgium.

Anderson was one of the sport's true all-rounders: he could climb well and still tough it out with the hardest of Belgian classics specialists. To use the Belgian term, he was a "Flahute"—a proper hardman. Anderson's victories included several one-day races and shorter stage races, such as the Tour Méditerranéen and the Critérium du Dauphiné Libéré; he also rode in thirteen Tours de France and finished second at the Tour of Flanders twice. He was one of the last generation of riders who could perform well in such early spring cobbled classics as Flanders and maintain their form for the later hilly ones, such as Liège–Bastogne–Liège; in 1983, he even won a particularly grueling edition of Amstel Gold after a hectic spring campaign. The spring events represent arguably the hardest block of racing on the professional calendar, so for Anderson to stay competitive throughout was no mean feat.

Perhaps his toughest and most successful year was 1985, when he won the Tour Méditerranéen, the Volta a Catalunya, the Critérium du Dauphiné Libéré, and the Tour of Switzerland—all after finishing second in the Tour of Flanders and Gent–Wevelgem. He even managed fifth place at the Tour de France. Results such as these underline his varied talent and are unlikely to be matched again. Ever. Anderson's down-to-earth approach to racing made him extremely popular, especially with the English-speaking media. After taking the yellow jersey in 1981, the straight-talking and phlegmatic Anderson famously said, "Great, now I don't have to wash my old jersey tonight: I'll get a new one."

1982:
Phil Anderson

"I was really committed when I left Australia for France [in 1980]. I had to be. I didn't have a huge contract or any big race wins, but Europe was where the racing was and I was passionate about it. And anyway, I would have done it for nothing. But like it or not, I was in Europe for the whole year, regardless of what happened. I mean, a plane ticket home in those days cost about what it does now, and back then that was a lot of money. Sure, I was lonely, but I just got on with it. Greg had already had some success before he turned pro, so he had a good contract to start with. I didn't even have the money to make a call back home. Not that Greg had it easy, though. Perhaps that's just the Aussie way: we just get on with it.

"The first time I met Greg was in 1979 when we were both young amateurs racing in the Red Zinger Classic [later known as the Coors Classic] in America. It was a week-long stage race, and the final stage was a criterium around North Boulder Park, Colorado. Anyway, I took a lap on the field [i.e. he lapped the other riders], and the crowd was getting really

1985 Gent–Wevelgem
Anderson's talents were nurtured throughout the 1980s by the likes of Peter Post, the uncompromising Dutch sports director, whose Raleigh and Panasonic squads were among the best of the period.

excited. Michael Aisner, the race organizer, was winding up the atmosphere over the PA, and he announced that if I could take a second lap, I'd get a $1,000 cash prize. Now, waving a huge pile of cash in front of me was a tremendous incentive, especially as I was already in the second attack of the race. And with me was none other than Greg LeMond. But a few laps from the finish in my crusade to take a second lap, Greg fell off. But he just got back up and chased, when he could have simply jumped back into the break. The regulations in bike racing say you can take a lap out in a criterium for crashes or mechanical problems, so if he'd taken his lap out and got back in with me and stayed with me he could have won that race overall. It was naive, but he was so fired up.

"Pros are meant to be these serious dogs—stoic characters and pretty intense about their racing. If they crack a smile on the podium it's something special."

"I turned pro the next year [1980], and although Greg was still amateur, I met him again at the pro-am Circuit de la Sarthe, which he won. Then I was there at his first win as a pro the following year, at the Tour de l'Oise, and I'll never forget it. We were in a late-stage breakaway with four or five others, and we came around the final corner, 300 meters before the finish. We were all pretty young and a bit disorganized, so we're all over the road and going full gas for the line, and Greg comes past us all on the outside to win. Right as he passes us, he raises his arms and, as he crosses the line, yells, 'Yee-hah!' I'd never heard anybody do that before. It was probably more memorable to me than it was for him, but pros are meant to be these serious dogs—stoic characters and pretty intense about their racing. If they crack a smile on the podium it's something special, and here was this young, spirited neo-pro showing some real emotion. It sure was enlightening.

"I went on and did reasonably well in the Tour [of 1981], winning a yellow jersey. It was nothing like Greg's achievements, but no non-European had worn the yellow jersey, so that was pretty big. It was a lot different then. As professionals, we'd race for 100 to 120 days a year; these days, they'll do 50 to 60. We all raced from February to October. I think Greg did a little less, especially as his career went on, but he probably raced around 80 to 90 days a year, and that's still way more than they do now.

"When I first went to Europe, I lived in Paris, and during the Tour de France, if you're not racing in it, there's not a lot going on there. So riders like Paul Sherwen and Graham Jones would tell me to go up to Belgium and race some kermesses. There's plenty of them and the people are friendly, so I went up there for a week or so and I loved it. Compared to my experiences [in Paris], people were far more friendly in Belgium, so I moved up there. It wasn't much of a move, because I didn't have much—just enough to fill a small car. I stayed in a guest house to start with, but by the end of 1980 I had an apartment in Lokeren.

"Greg obviously missed the American life in Europe. Guimard wanted to keep an eye on him, so the team had him living in Nantes. But if Greg had two weeks off, he'd go home to America. He'd come up to Belgium for races too, though, and he clearly preferred it there. They spoke English and had English TV, and you can get quite homesick, so he and Kathy moved to Kortrijk in West Flanders. By then I was living in Waregem—the neighboring town—and Kathy and my wife at the time, Anne, got on pretty well. Greg and I were really close mates in those early years. Depending on the schedule, we would go to some races together, even though we were on separate teams, and usually in an average week we'd train three or four times together too. This was old-school training, though, based on how you felt, so no heart-rate monitors; you'd be lucky to have a speedo. So we'd do some long, hard rides—five or six hours.

"On training days I'd ride over to his place and he'd still be walking around in his pajamas. If he was just back from a trip, his suitcase would be upside down and there'd be stuff all over the floor. And he would always have lost something: an arm warmer, his helmet . . . But that was Greg. He even got on the wrong plane once and ended up in the wrong place for a race, managing to get the plane to Florida rather than Virginia. He eventually turned up the next day, on the morning of the race. That sort of thing was pretty regular. He wasn't always the most organized rider; he always arrived flying by the seat of his pants. I'm not sure you could get away with that stuff these days, but despite all that he still managed to get some pretty good results.

"Of course he had a massive engine, and he could set a goal and give everything for that. He'd always arrive at the events he targeted physically ready to perform. He was possibly the first to do that, but unlike most he really could deliver. Sure, sometimes at races he'd be at the back having a laugh, but it was always with another goal in mind, a way down the line. We'd often do training camps in Spain for the World Championships. He would be so focused, and would prepare meticulously for ten days solid. He could never be underestimated either: he'd often be in a race he hadn't even been considered for and then he'd do well.

"They'd painted the road with my name in yellow, and they gave me the key to the town for the day. They wanted to know all about this kid from Australia."

"We were treated so well in Belgium, and still are: it's a part of their culture there. Sure, it's a big sport in France, but in Belgium, and especially West Flanders, they just live and breathe the sport of cycling. When I first got the jersey at the Tour, most people didn't know where Australia was even, so when I was interviewed after a stage I'd always say that I lived in Lokeren. The Belgian journos loved that, and obviously all the local newspapers that reported on the race picked up on it, so when I got [back to Lokeren] everyone came out for a reception in the town square. They'd painted the road with my name in yellow, and they gave me the key to the town for the day. They wanted to know all about this kid from Australia. They just loved the fact that I lived in the town and had put Belgium back on the Tour de France map, even if it was just for one day.

"A couple of years later, in 1983, we all went to the Kortrijk town center for Greg when he won the World Championships. There was a huge to-do, with a big stage in the town square; Eddy Merckx and Briek Schotte were there too. The Belgians really embraced both of us as a part of the local community. They obviously wished we were Belgian, but cycling is so massive in West Flanders, and to have someone winning the Tour or the World Championships is huge. I mean, even just having a local professional is regarded as good, so having a successful one living locally is treated with a huge sense of pride. It was always easy to get stuff done, and people around would always go out of their way to help you. I moved back to France later in my career [in the late 1990s], but I still have many good friends in Belgium, and people still fondly remember what we did.

"Cycling was very much a blue-collar sport when Greg and I came into it. By the time I came out of cycling, it was slowly turning a little bit more beige than blue. It's still not quite white, but it's long been through the bleach since the early days. The day after the Tour de France in 1981, for example, I had this meeting with the team [Peugeot] to discuss the following year's deal. I'd got myself a manager. I mean, it was the same company that represented some Formula 1 drivers, and so in cycling this was a pretty bold move. The management company were saying to the bosses that the team hadn't had a leader like me for ten years, and that [Peugeot the company] was a multimillion dollar business. I remember them saying all this, and then saying, 'And you're offering him what my secretary is paid.' My lawyer got me an extra $1,000 a month. It was headline news in the papers the next day—not the money, but because I'd used a representative to negotiate a 'big new contract.'

"Things were changing. Greg and his dad, Bob, had both helped me and given me more confidence in negotiations. Previously, there were no negotiations in cycling, and definitely no representatives. After that, my teammates started asking me how I did it. They had always said that they would just take what they got, wait until the end of the season, and leave it up to the team. Greg had a lot to do with changing that, and he was always saying to the other riders how far behind American sports cycling was. All that started to change when Guimard went over to America with Hinault to sign Greg's first contract. So in some ways it's all Guimard's fault!"

1985 Tour de France
Early Oakley eyeshades at the 1985 Tour. It was thanks to Greg, Phil Anderson, Andy Hampsten, and other, mostly English-speaking riders of the 1980s professional peloton that this style of sunglasses became so popular.

Team: Renault-Elf-Gitane

1st: Tour de l'Avenir
1st: stages 4, 5, and 8
3rd: points classification and stage 10
5th: stage 3

2nd: Tour Méditerranéen
4th: stage 4

2nd: UCI Road World Championships (Goodwood, England)

3rd: Grand Prix de Rennes

3rd: Tirreno-Adriatico
1st: stage 3
5th: stage 5

3rd: Tour of Corsica
3rd: stage 3
5th: stage 2

12th: Gent-Wevelgem

13th: Tour of Luxembourg

15th: Critérium International
5th: time trial

17th: Milan-San Remo

23rd: Tour de l'Aude

35th: Paris-Brussels

Grand Prix Eddy Merckx
7th: points race
12th: derny-paced race

Renault-Elf-Gitane team presentation
The Renault team of 1982 boasted an embarrassment of riches: Laurent Fignon, Bernard Hinault, Marc Madiot, and Greg.

"Cyrille Guimard was the best coach I ever had. I had a lot of good coaches, but I never took any coach's word [as read]. *I* became my best coach."

Greg LeMond

Tour de l'Avenir

This was the first of Greg's many wins in France with Guimard at the helm. The Brèton was a fierce competitor as a racer, and became one of the greatest directors the sport has ever seen.

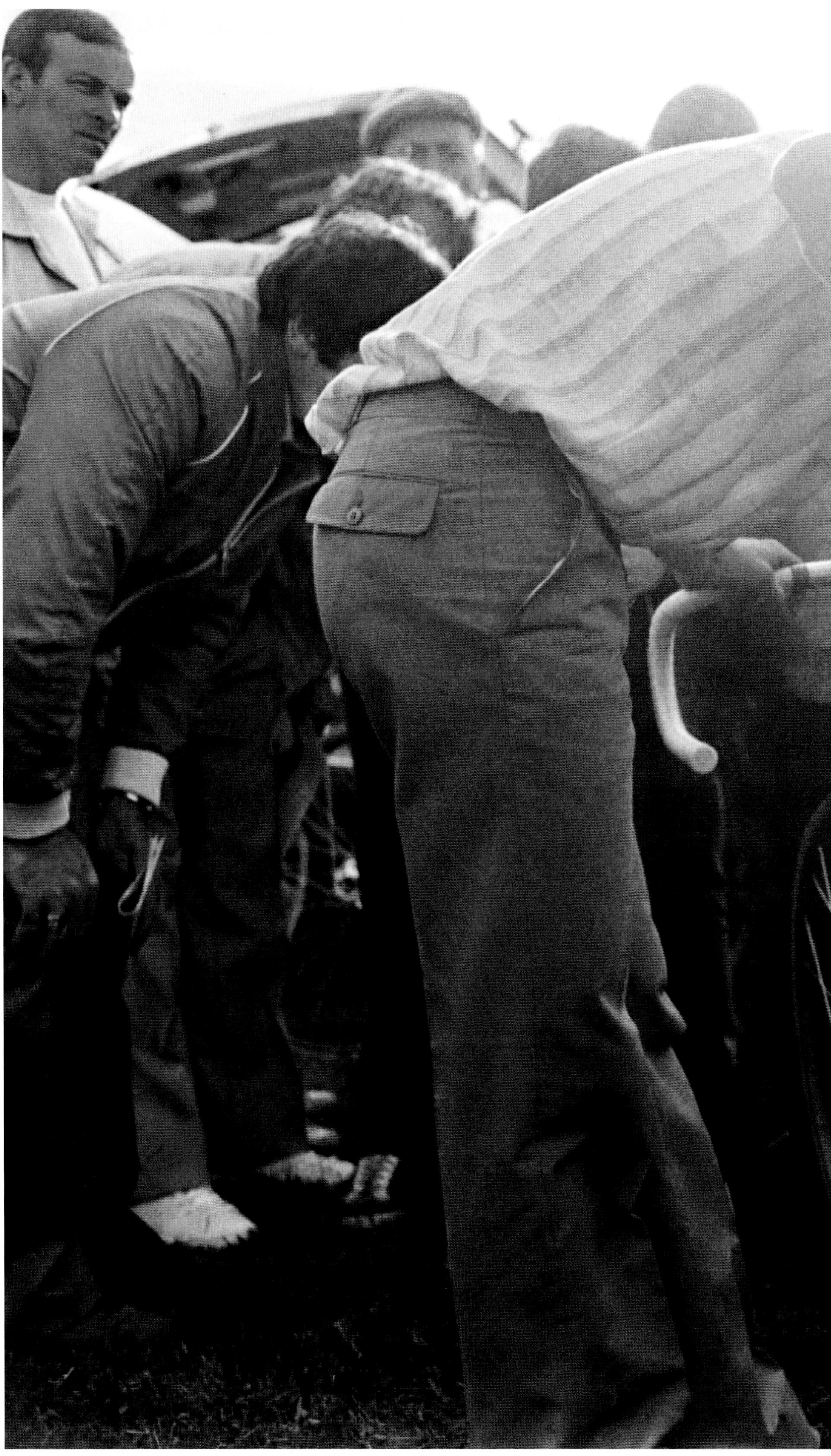

Saint-Brieuc
Some of the post-Tour criteriums consisted of exhibition races, while some were almost novelty events. Here, for example, Bernard Hinault helps Greg set up a team track bike ready for an event at a velodrome.

RENAULT

ABOVE, TOP **Gent-Wevelgem**
Climbing the infamous cobbled Kemmelberg at the Gent-Wevelgem. This semi-classic has always been regarded as a hardman's race, with riders often having to contend with bad weather and strong winds. It's a midweek warm-up race before the Tour of Flanders. Greg finished twelfth in 1982, winning the bunch sprint. A few weeks later, he broke his collarbone at Liège-Bastogne-Liège and had to sit out the remainder of the spring races.

"To start with in France, we had no friends, no house, no furniture, no money—nothing. We didn't speak French and there were no American movies on TV. In those days, there wasn't a McDonald's, so you couldn't just go into Nantes and get a cheeseburger to remind you of home. There were only three television stations, which were [usually] showing French political debates. So you read a book, or you sat around the house. My first month or two I read a dozen or so Robert Ludlum books. OK, I thought, that's enough."

Greg LeMond

"In my first year, we'd escape to Belgium and I'd do a few races and training rides there. The first year, we spent four weeks in a hotel while I was racing: Het Volk, all the preparation for the Tour of Flanders, and then Paris-Roubaix and Flèche Wallonne, Liège . . . So, after four weeks we said, let's move here; I can even go home between races. But when people in France heard we were moving to Belgium, it felt as if we were telling the French public that I didn't like their country. But Belgium had the advantage of living in Europe and being able to talk some English, which kept me sane. We really liked living in Belgium."

Greg LeMond

OPPOSITE, BOTTOM, AND ABOVE

Tour de l'Avenir

By the end of the race, Greg was more than ten minutes ahead of his nearest rivals: the Scot Robert Millar, and rising Colombian climbing star Luis Herrera. On the mountainous stage 5, Greg beat Millar solo by more than five minutes.

UCI Road World Championships, Goodwood, England
After 18 laps and 276 kilometers, the contenders for the podium formed an elite group, with some showing signs of tiredness. From left: Michel Pollentier (Belgium), Joop Zoetemelk (Netherlands, finished fourth), Juan Fernández Martín (Spain), Greg, Marc Madiot (France), Jan Raas (Netherlands), Giuseppe Saronni (Italy, winner), and Sean Kelly (Ireland, third).

UCI Road World Championships, Goodwood, England

In the final kilometers, Jonathan "Jock" Boyer attacks the remaining group of favorites and establishes a gap. It isn't a big gap, but races have been won from similar situations. Behind, the group is taken by surprise and initially hesitates. Eventually, Greg rides to the front and appears to take up the chase . . . For one teammate to chase another teammate is unheard of in cycling, and watching this finale in retrospect doesn't lessen the controversy. Cycling is about racing as a team, and Greg's actions were (and still are) regarded as a no-no. There was an explanation, however, albeit a slightly bizarre one.

The idea, according to the team's management, had been to run the race as a sort of US championships—a race within a race—so any tactical ideas that the Americans had for the event clearly didn't include the possibility that the team might win. Whatever the team's thinking, it didn't look good from the outside, and Greg was openly criticized.

If the strategy had been to ride as a team, the outcome might have been different. Boyer believed that he would have won if Greg hadn't chased him in the final kilometer, but at the end of a gruelling World Championships it was neither much of a breakaway nor much of a chase. In opening up the sprint early, Greg probably hurt his own chances of winning more than anything else. In a sprint like that, it's all about catching the right wheel at the right time.

It's all academic anyway, because everybody missed Giuseppe Saronni's explosive jump for the line, and he'd have won regardless. All the American pair managed to do was weaken their own positions: Boyer's attack was both too early to win solo and too late to drag out a chase from their exhausted rivals, and Greg's response was premature, naive even. By their own admission, they were simply watching each other and not the opposition.

Greg rarely shows his competitive side in a petulant manner, but this time was different. Fully aware of what he was doing, he let his feelings be known by saying to the press afterwards, "We agreed that Greg LeMond was racing for Greg LeMond and that Jock Boyer was racing for Jock Boyer. I'm racing for Renault and I'm racing for myself. It's a business and it's my living. To me, that second place was almost as good as winning, especially at my age."

In the final analysis, it was the first medal for an American at a World Championships, and Greg was certainly a surprise addition to the podium. It marked the beginning of his career-long battle for the medals with the likes of Sean Kelly, Stephen Roche, and numerous Italians. That silver of 1982, however, was a hard lesson learned: Saronni had been unstoppable.

RENAULT elf

"That's bike racing: you wouldn't expect a team leader at the Tour de France to just roll over for you. Not when you're a Frenchman at the Tour de France—not even if you're not a Frenchman."

SEAN KELLY

PREVIOUS SPREAD

Tour of Lombardy

"In 1983, the Super Prestige award [see page 84] came down to the Tour of Lombardy. I was leading the standings, but if Kelly won the Tour and I was worse than fifth, he would win the award. In the finale, I realized there were a few alliances going on, with [Francesco] Moser and some of the Italians. I was second to Kelly in the sprint, but that was the final race and it was enough to hold on to the lead overall."

Greg LeMond

ABOVE

1984 Liège–Bastogne–Liège

As is often the case in a late-spring classic, the group at the end of this 246 km race was a quality one. Greg, Sean Kelly, Laurent Fignon and Phil Anderson were all there to fight it out in the finale. Kelly was the eventual winner, with Anderson in second place and Greg in third.

New Kids on the Block

When Sean Kelly turned professional in 1977, cycling was a very different sport from the one we know today. With its impenetrable language and customs, it required an apprenticeship that, even for a French national, was tough. Such talented "foreigners" as Kelly had to be that much better and that much more motivated than their French counterparts even to make it onto a professional team. Kelly wasn't the first Irishman—or the first English-speaker, for that matter—to ride as a continental pro, but he was certainly one of the first to do rather well at it.

In the 1980s, with victories in nine Monument classics and countless stages and jerseys to his name, Kelly was often ranked as the world's number one road racer. When it came to one-day races, very few riders have been as good as Kelly. He owed his success not only to his ability, which was undoubted, but also to his phlegmatic, no-nonsense approach to bike racing, which won him many friends in the peloton. He wasn't the bossy, aggressive, patron-like figure played by Bernard Hinault, but neither was he the charismatic and likable joker, a role taken by Greg. Rather, Kelly was a much more elusive and laid-back character, seemingly unruffled by anything. Indeed, he was so nonchalant during press conferences and interviews that it was often nigh-on impossible to get him to say anything quote-worthy at all. But his rivals, adversaries, and peers respected him all the more for it.

As a rider, Kelly was far more than just a talented sprinter. He also had a knack for knowing exactly when a race was about to fragment, or exactly when to bridge across to a dangerous breakaway before the finale. What's more, he always made it look effortless. Robert Millar said of Kelly that, "Sure, there were riders who were as hard as he was, there were riders as fast as he was, and there were riders as talented as he was, but for me there was no one who had all those characteristics and did the job of a professional bike rider so well. Start of season to end of season, barely a dip in form and never a decline in how tough he was." In the peloton, the riders called him "King Kelly," perhaps rightly so.

Whenever Kelly and Greg went head to head, they'd invariably end up on the podium, or thereabouts. Throughout the 1980s, the two men dominated the racing, especially when the going was hard, long, and hilly, in which case you could always expect to see them in the finale. In fact, there were very few pure road racers as good or as well matched. In the 1983 Tour of Lombardy, for example, Kelly came in first with Greg in second place; in the Liège-Bastogne-Liège of 1984, Kelly was first again with Greg third; and in the 1985 Paris–Roubaix, a long, hard, and brutally tough race, Kelly finished third and Greg fourth. Longer stage races were out of Kelly's reach, so he chased other objectives, winning the green jersey (points classification) at the Tour de France four times, in 1982, 1983, 1985, and 1989; he also won the intermediate sprints classification three times, as well as five individual stages. Despite not being regarded as a Grand Tour contender, Kelly still managed to win the Vuelta a España in 1988, the points classification four times, and sixteen individual stages—proof, if any was needed, that he wasn't "just" a sprinter.

At the shorter stage races, Kelly was unstoppable, winning the Tour of Switzerland and the Volta a Catalunya twice, the Tour of the Basque Country and the Critérium International three times, and his home-country tour, the Nissan Classic (also known as the Tour of Ireland), four times. Kelly's record of seven wins at the first big stage race of the season, Paris–Nice, ran consecutively, from 1982 to 1988. These tough season-openers cemented his early season form, setting him up for the spring classics. It was at the one-day Monuments, however, that Kelly truly shined. His palmares for these races

speak for themselves: winner of the Tour of Lombardy three times; Milan–San Remo, Paris–Roubaix and Liège–Bastogne–Liège twice; and Gent–Wevelgem and the Tour of Flanders once.

In 1983, Kelly was the odds-on favorite to win the World Championships in Altenrhein, Switzerland. Earlier that summer, while Greg sat it out, Kelly had a great Tour de France, winning the green jersey in Paris and coming into the form of his life. So, when they met at Altenrhein, perhaps he underestimated Greg's talent as a rider, or maybe he thought he'd tire and relent. Whatever his reasons for losing to Greg that year, Kelly (who finished eighth) rarely let the American out of his sight in the single-day races that followed. After Greg's victory, they would clash time and time again for the next decade.

The competitiveness between the two riders was matched by a mutual respect, especially after the 1989 World Championships, when Greg was credited with saying, "I felt bad for Sean. I mean, it was like, 'Oh man! If I can't win I want Kelly to win.' But it was also very satisfying to actually have beaten him. In 1983, I was so close to getting him at Lombardy. And then in 1986 at Milan–San Remo and Paris–Roubaix, I was with him, but I was no contest for him in the sprint. I just didn't have anything in my legs. He just blew by me." Kelly came so close to victory at the World Championships on so many occasions—as Greg always came close to winning at the Monuments—that the American famously once said to the Irishman, "I'll trade you a Worlds title for a Paris–Roubaix."

1983: Sean Kelly

"We'd already heard a lot about Greg after he'd won the Tour de l'Avenir—word had gotten back to us in the peloton that Cyrille Guimard had found this amazing young American rider and signed him for Renault. I liked Greg a lot, despite the fact that we were always opponents in races and always billed as big rivals by the press. We'd always been good friends.

"In the races, especially when the chips were down, it was always very aggressive between us, but after the race I got on very well with Greg. We never had any big fights either during or outside the race. And I suppose the English-speaking [factor] was a big part of that. When I joined Flandria-Velda, the manager, Jean de Gribaldy, couldn't speak a word of English, and the personnel in the team spoke no English either. There were a few riders like Marcel Tinazzi who spoke pretty good English . . . Those guys would help out when I was in trouble, when we were talking about the race, which, to be fair, wasn't a lot in those days. We didn't have these big team briefings where the DS [directeur sportif] would be looking through the route manual and going through every kilometer—that wasn't the case back then. You would only talk about the race a little bit. I was there with my mouth open at times; they would make a comment in English to make me aware of what they were talking about.

"In my situation—and it happened so many times—the guys don't want to ride with you, especially if you are good in the sprint. With Greg, it was the same situation."

"Although, when you're in a race situation in a move with five people [such as a small breakaway], there isn't a huge amount of conversation between the riders, except if you have two riders from the same team or country. But in general, you wouldn't have a lot of discussion or conversation with your fellow breakaway riders. The tactics in bike racing are pretty straightforward in the end, especially in the sprint. The biggest problem would be if you're in the final in a big peloton, getting ready for the sprint. The language barrier there can be a bit of a problem, because when they shout something to you, it's more difficult [to understand them].

"At Milan–San Remo in 1986, I realized the danger when Greg attacked late on. The Italian Mario Beccia had attacked, and Greg went with him, or went after him, and then I was in a group with a lot of the other favorites, such as [Eric] Vanderaerden, who had been following me throughout the day before we got to the Poggio [Vanderaerden was one of Kelly's career-long nemeses]. Just before the top, I started messing about and pretending that my gears were slipping, so Vanderaerden and the rest of the group came past me. Then I went on the attack, from behind them, in the last 700 or 800 meters . . . I got across to Greg and made the descent with Beccia. Beccia was the one who started riding a bit at the bottom of the Poggio descent, because he realized it was the chance of a lifetime for him to get a result, to get on the podium at a Milan–San Remo. I was always hesitant about riding, because Greg can be very strong in the sprint. The three of us made it to the finish and, in the end, I just had a bit more than Greg left in the tank.

"Of course, whenever I was with Greg in the final [the last few hundred meters before the finishing line], it was always at the end of a difficult race. In Milan–San Remo, you had the Cipressa and Poggio climbs at the end, after almost 300 kilometers. The World Championships would also be on a very difficult circuit, and always over 250 kilometers and around seven hours, so when you get into the final with a small number of riders, the race always keeps going full gas.

"It's a different situation if you get into a final with a group of ten or fifteen riders. Take a stage in the Tour de France, for example: it would always be a difficult final as a lot of guys are not going to ride. In my situation—and it happened so many times—the guys don't want to ride with you, especially if you are good in the sprint. With Greg, it was the same situation: in a small group, he was really good in the sprint—even in the bunch sprints he was really good—but he never really tried his best in the big sprints. He knew he wasn't going to win, but he would have been capable of being in the top five. He probably realized that to win the bunch sprints, on the flat with the big sprinters there . . . he probably realized that he was just a little bit off that pace to win. He would say, what's the point of getting into all that risk just to finish second, or third, or fifth? He had other fish to fry. In a stage race, he was always capable of winning. And certainly, in the Tour de France or the bigger races, he had much more important things [to do] than get into that mix-up of danger for little gain.

"Back then, [the Tour] was probably a bit easier than it is now, because today the race is much more

1984 Liège-Bastogne-Liège
Sean Kelly won fourteen races in the first seven weeks of the 1984 season.

competitive in the different disciplines. In the sprint, you have these big lead-out trains, and that's something that has been going on for a long time. The sprints have become more specialized. In the mountains and the time trials, it's probably just that bit faster overall. So it's difficult for guys to do everything and as well. But they don't have to do it all: are you concentrating on sprints? Or are you concentrating on stage victories?

"I probably didn't say it [at the time], but I had a bit of doubt that I could make the podium or win the Tour de France outright. It was always going to be difficult for me."

"In Greg's case, he was a big favorite, so when he got to that level to win the Tour de France, he'd always be marked. Whereas for me, I was one of the favorites too but would have been a second-tier favorite to win the race. I was winning the Tour of Switzerland and Paris–Nice and a lot of other stage races, and I proved I could do well on the Tour de France, coming fourth [in 1985], but my objectives would have been different from Greg's: I was going for stages and sprinting in the stages. The green jersey was certainly my biggest target, and in the general classification I was up there as well. And I probably didn't say it [at the time], but I had a bit of doubt that I could make the podium or win the Tour de France outright. It was always going to be difficult for me.

"Greg and I were always competitors. Later, when I moved to PDM and Greg was challenging to win the Tour, we had guys like [Steven] Rooks and [Gert-Jan] Theunisse and other guys who were challenging. I remember there was an occasion on that Tour when he won with team Z [in 1990]—he had a problem on one of the stages. There was a mountain not so far from the finish, maybe thirty or forty kilometers, and he had a flat on the descent. And I remember he was a little bit behind because it was very, very fast racing, I found myself in a group with Greg, but he was chasing, and out front there was [Claudio] Chiappucci and Theunisse and a lot of the other favorites. Greg said to me, he asked me could I ride with him? But I had Theunisse, my teammate, out in front, so it wasn't possible at all.

"[Hinault] really did push Greg in the Tour; he didn't make it easy for him. I think that Greg was expecting, as promised, that he would have to work for it, and then it would be his turn. But it didn't turn out to be as easy for him. In the peloton at the time, we had no idea what was actually happening . . . I don't think Greg realized it was happening until it happened out there on the road. And that was the same for all of us, because the spat [within the La Vie Claire team] went on behind the scenes. We learned about it a long time later.

"That's bike racing: you wouldn't expect a team leader at the Tour de France to just roll over for you. Not when they're a Frenchman at the Tour de France—not even if they're not a Frenchman. But you understand that in the professional circuit, when you're in teams . . . I remember in some of the classics, like the Ardennes classics, there were rivals who were all hoping to do well, and then sometimes your teammates can become your biggest rivals. I didn't have to wait until out on the road and physically see it; I knew in the early part of the season [it was happening]. You don't expect that in the early part of a season, but things unfold . . . your tactics might have to change. In a Tour, however, it gets more complicated: the pressures work on you over the three weeks, maybe not in the early days but certainly in the final week or ten days of racing. You know that, if there's an opportunity, he will push you and test you, and that's what Greg had to go through with Hinault.

"It was just a situation where Greg was in a French team with French management: all of that was going to work against him. In those days, it was more difficult being a foreigner in a foreign team because you were always looked at as the foreigner. And I think they were definitely going to work against you if the situation suited and benefited the team . . . That was the scenario Greg was in. But that's changed: nationalities are put to one side nowadays. If you're capable of performing well, teams are behind you 100 percent.

"Back then, the problem was my program of races. In terms of the Tour de France, I probably raced too many other races before the Tour; if I'd been in another team, then it would have changed. First of all, though, it comes down to constitution—the way you are. Other riders would not have been able to support the amount of racing I was doing; my program was totally crazy. Compared to now, we were doing a huge number of races. Also, the DS was always telling me, 'You can't be tired from too much racing. Don't listen to the journalists as they will make you tired mentally. But physically, you can't get tired.'

"And you had to enjoy the racing. Maybe you didn't show that for the main part, but you had to be enjoying it. I don't think anything would keep you in there if you weren't enjoying it. There were a lot of times when you were tested, because it's such a bloody hard sport. Even more so back in our day,

as you weren't looked after as well. Whereas now, the athletes are treated much better. From my point of view, some parts—the training, the horrible weather—there were times when you went through difficult patches, but I enjoyed quite a lot of it.

"You had to enjoy the racing. Maybe you didn't show that for the main part, but you had to be enjoying it. I don't think anything would keep you in there if you weren't enjoying it."

1983 UCI Road World Championships, Altenrhein, Switzerland
Greg's win was emphatic, but there would be other head-to-heads between him and Kelly. Greg often joked that he'd gladly swap a Worlds title for one of Kelly's Monument wins.

"The 1989 World Championships [in which Kelly finished third]—it all came down to the final two laps on that circuit in Chambèry. It was a difficult climb, and some were just about surviving, whereas others wanted to go on the attack. Rooks was already out in front with a few others when Laurent Fignon went on the attack; he went first and Greg followed. Then there was a lot of changing—guys going forward and coming back. From my point of view, I knew on the second-to-last time on the climb that I was in a bit of difficulty, so the plan was to just get over the climb as best I could, especially on the last lap. I remember when Fignon attacked and Greg went after him, I wasn't able to follow them; I couldn't react. Then I got to the top of the climb and [sighs] I made the descent and got back with just a kilometer to go . . .

"People always ask me, would I swap a World Championships for a Monument, and I recall a conversation I had with Greg about it . . . And joking aside, without doubt, we'd both swap! The World Championships was the sort of race I was always very powerful and strong in, but I never managed to pull off a win. I've no resentment towards Greg, though; he always rode a very good race. He never had a team around him like the big cycling nations.

"Greg never got an easy World Championships."

Team: Renault-Elf-Gitane

1st: As à Genève (post-World Championships)

1st: Critérium du Dauphiné Libéré
1st: stages 1, 5 and 7b
4th: stage 6
5th: prologue and stage 4

1st: Super Prestige Pernod (season-long points-based award)

1st: UCI Road World Championships (Altenrhein, Switzerland)

2nd: Cluses (post-Tour criterium, France)

2nd: Grand Prix des Nations

2nd: Hoevelaken (post-Tour criterium, Netherlands)

2nd: Tour of Lombardy

3rd: Eindhoven (post-Tour criterium, Netherlands)

3rd: Schijndel (post-Tour criterium, Netherlands)

3rd: Valkenburg (post-Tour criterium, Netherlands)

4th: Blois-Chaville

4th: Tour of Switzerland
2nd: stages 1 and 3
3rd: stages 4 and 7
5th: prologue and stage 2

8th: Baracchi Trophy (team time trial with Pascal Poisson)

10th: La Flèche Wallonne

10th: Tirreno-Adriatico

12th Gent-Wevelgem

12th: Paris-Brussels

30th: Milan-San Remo

31st: Tour of Holland
3rd: stage 1a
5th: stage 2

78th: Liège-Bastogne-Liège

Grand Prix Eddy Merckx
6th: derny-paced race

Tour Méditerranéen
1st: stage 1

Tour of Sardinia
5th: stage 4

Vuelta a España
2nd: stage 15
4th: stage 12
Abandoned stage 17

1981 Renault-Elf-Gitane team photo
This was the year in which Greg joined the Renault team. It was packed with champions and talent for several years, a consistency that added to its success.

Kathy and Greg at Château-Chinon, France

"Psychologically, 1983 was a hard year. We were homesick much of the time, the weather was bad, and I seemed to be always sick. In those days, we trained at way too much volume. Coming from the US, it was different cold viruses that knocked me back [at the Vuelta a España that year, Greg was suffering from bronchitis]. I was usually dying to get home, and by September I was done."

Greg LeMond

RENAULT
elf
elf
CYCLES

Tour Méditerranéen
The "superteam" of 1983. From left: Greg, Laurent Fignon, Lucien Didier, and Dominique Gaigne.

Critérium du Dauphiné Libéré: stage 7
Greg climbs one of the toughest and loneliest mountains in cycle racing: the desolate moonscape of Mont Ventoux. It was a decisive stage in the end, with Greg being dropped by Pascal Simon after a lengthy duel. The American clung on to the time gap, no doubt encouraged by the ever-present Guimard.

ABOVE, TOP **"We raced brilliantly in '83: Hinault raced for people, and I raced for people. It was so different being on my own; I didn't have someone telling me to hold back or not chase somebody."**

Greg LeMond

ABOVE **Vuelta a España**
The Vuelta was a spring race in 1983, providing an early test for those with Tour de France ambitions. Renault had quite a team that year, with Greg, Fignon, and Hinault. Greg was ill and out of sorts, however, abandoning the race on stage 17. Fignon was the eventual winner, becoming favorite for the Tour in July.

Critérium du Dauphiné Libéré: stage 7

On the bottom section of Mont Ventoux, Greg was outgunned by Simon (seen here behind Greg) and Robert Millar, Simon's teammate at Peugeot. The three would make up the podium, although Simon later failed a drugs test, making Greg the winner. More important than victory, however, were Greg's three emphatic stage wins, which made quite an impact.

"In 1983, I should have done the Tour because Fignon won it. I was fourth in the Tour of Switzerland and winner of the Dauphiné. Guimard asked me to do the Tour, but we agreed not to do it until the following year. It was probably one of the biggest mistakes I made: with Hinault out [I could've won]."

Greg LeMond

Château-Chinon
The post-Tour de France criterium at Château-Chinon. Despite sitting out the Tour in 1983, Greg competed in several of the post-Tour criteriums and did well. Regardless of their status as exhibition races, they still provided a tough challenge, with the Tour riders on top form after three weeks on the road. They also paid well.

"I had a training regime for the Tour and the World Championships: overload the system. It's just basic physiology—overload the system and make a full recovery, and it will really make you strong at that level. If you don't fully recover, you can easily ride yourself into the ground and be slightly overtrained all the time. I was really good at never doing that, and was always fully recovered when I was training."

Greg LeMond

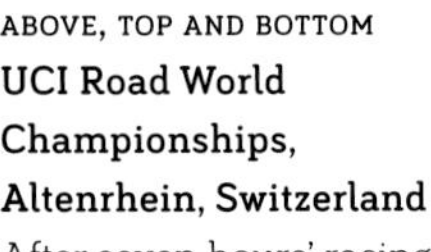

ABOVE, TOP AND BOTTOM

UCI Road World Championships, Altenrhein, Switzerland

After seven hours' racing on a brutal circuit around the Swiss town of Altenrhein, Greg won solo by just over a minute from Adri van der Poel and Stephen Roche.

"I had a terrible night's sleep the night before the Worlds. I was so nervous that I threw up my breakfast. Guimard came up to me before the start of the race and said, 'Greg, you're going to do really well today. Before their best days, all great champions have a sleepless night—because they know they can win.'"

Greg LeMond

UCI Road World Championships, Altenrhein, Switzerland

"I was just floating. With thirty-eight kilometers to go, Robert Millar attacked the peloton at the perfect time, so I went away after him. Moreno Argentin and a couple of others followed [only Spanish climber Faustino Rupérez managed to hold on at the bell for the final lap, eventually finishing fourth]. Argentin hated me after that day. He got so much crap from the Italians for working with me and then getting dropped that he took it out on me. He pretty much marked me out of the race in Barcelona in 1984. Then in 1985, neither of us would chase [Joop] Zoetemelk . . ."

Greg LeMond

Blois–Chaville

Greg rides alongside teammate and soon-to-be rival Laurent Fignon at the race that's now known as Paris–Tours. Despite it being the season-ending race in France, Greg needed to put in a good performance in order to stay in the hunt for the now-defunct Super Prestige Pernod award, given to the rider with the most number of points at the end of the season. Greg finished the race in fourth, with Belgian Ludo Peeters taking the win.

ABOVE, TOP **Blois–Chaville**
Greg was in demand from all quarters. Here, he is congratulated on his victory at the World Championships by former Tour de France winner Bernard Thévenet, who was working for the La Redoute team at the time.

ABOVE **Paris–Brussels**
Despite the illnesses and grueling travel program, 1983 underlined Greg's ability and consistency. He demonstrated that he could compete at the sharp end of any race, from spring to autumn. His victory at the World Championships seemed to add confidence to his racing too, with twelfth at a rain-soaked Paris–Brussels being a hard-earned end-of-season result.

ABOVE, TOP Kortrijk, Belgium
Greg and Kathy with Bob and Bertha LeMond at the reception held for Greg in Kortrijk after he won the World Championships. The cycle-racing fans in his adopted hometown in Belgium gave Greg far more support, attention, and accolades than he'd have received in Nevada.

ABOVE Presentation for 1984 Tour de France, Paris
The presentation for the following year's Tour de France, and Hinault is back. He wasn't quite at his best, but he was definitely back—and holding the map. The Renault team would start the year favorites to win the race, and even Laurent Fignon manages a smile. Perhaps he knew something the others didn't . . .

"I realized that wearing the Worlds jersey has a psychological effect on you. Once you win it, you have opportunities to make money, and you do. But people want you to do stuff, and all that stuff takes energy; it takes everything away. It's like you're worn down."

Greg LeMond

ABOVE **Super Prestige Pernod Awards, Paris**

A motley crew, including Cyrille Guimard in black tie, stand behind the winners at the Super Pernod Prestige awards dinner in Paris. Standing next to Guimard (from left) are rugby player Jean-Pierre Rives; Miss France 1983, Isabelle Turpault; American singer and songwriter Mort Shuman; actor Jacques Weber; an unknown guest; actress Marion Game; French TV host Michel Drucker; and singer Enrico Macias. Seated (from left) are riders Steven Rooks, Gilbert Duclos-Lassalle, Greg, and Laurent Fignon.

170

"I still tell young people the same thing: what the sport of cycling is about is a sense of freedom. You can ride anywhere and see what's around the corner."

RON KIEFEL

PREVIOUS SPREAD
Tour de France
Following a crash caused by an overzealous spectator, Greg leaves the Italian Roberto Visentini on the floor.

ABOVE Coors Classic
Ron Kiefel (left) shares a joke with fellow American Andy Weaver on the starting line.

From a Piece of Cake to Holy Cow!

Ron Kiefel was another rider nurtured by Eddie Borysewicz and his fledgling US cycling system. Ron had ridden with Greg in the junior national time trial squad, netting a bronze medal at world junior level in 1978—an achievement he would repeat at senior level at the Olympics in 1984. With three gold medals at the 1983 US National Road Race Championships—a clean sweep of all the road-based events—Ron was earning a reputation as a rider with a good turn of speed and a head for racing, making him a well-known figure in American cycling. His Olympics success was followed by a ten-year professional career, completing the Tour de France six times and taking stage wins at the Giro d'Italia and the Coors Classic. A founding member of the 7-Eleven team, Ron became the first American to win a stage at a Grand Tour when he won stage 15 of the 1985 Giro d'Italia.

Exactly what the Italians thought of the 7-Eleven team when they touched down on Italian soil in 1985 remains unknown. Many of the team had raced abroad before, some having had success in amateur races in France and Belgium, but Italian professional cycling was different. Very different. The peloton wasn't the most welcoming environment for the new boys either, with many of the local riders blaming them for crashes or accusing them of just "being in the way." But they had talent, added some color—and had a lot of fun. They had morale too, something that many of the rival teams' more serious sporting directors struggled to maintain. The "bad riding" accusations were, it seems, based on jealousy.

When Ron won the Trofeo Laigueglia, a hilly, early season one-day race in Liguria, Italy, the team was barely weeks into its first European campaign. But with this surprise win, the 7-Eleven team had quickly and very properly arrived on the professional scene. The Trofeo wasn't a huge race, but, coming as it did at the start of the season, it was a significant one—a race used by the major teams to try out their big guns. The list of previous winners read like a who's who of professional cycling: Eddy Merckx, Roger De Vlaeminck, Michele Dancelli, Italo Zilioli, Guiseppe Saronni, to name but a few. So the addition of Kiefel's name was quite a coup. It also secured the team's invite to that year's Giro d'Italia, at which Ron would win again. They'd gone from peloton whipping boys to respected racers in a matter of months.

Despite making only a cursory appearance on the professional racing calendar, in 1989 and 1990, the Tour de Trump—named after the larger-than-life American tycoon—made cycling history. Trump boasted that it would become as big as the Tour de France, but after two years and $750,000 in costs, he pulled out. The 1990 edition was won by the Mexican Raúl Alcalá, and the race became known as the Tour DuPont. The prize money at stake, almost as much as offered by the Tour de France, meant that many riders from Europe traveled across the Atlantic to have a stab at the jackpot. When the 7-Eleven team decided to use aero (triathlon) handlebars at the 1989 Tour de Trump, Ron, a useful team rider against the clock, became one of the first pro cyclists to win a time trial at a professional cycling race using such 'bars, with 7-Eleven's Dag Otto Lauritzen of Norway netting the $50,000 first prize. The significance of these events for Greg's 1989 Tour de France campaign was immense.

This American success had begun a decade earlier with those junior-team bronze medals at the World Championships of 1978 and 1979. Jeff Bradley, Greg Demgen, Alexi Grewal, Andy Hampsten, Roy Knickman, Davis Phinney, Thurlow Rogers, Doug Shapiro, and Ron were all on the US national team in 1984 when it traveled to Europe in the spring and won more than half the races it entered. A year later, these same riders would form the basis of the newly professional team aiming for the Tour de France.

1984:
Ron Kiefel

"My parents rode bikes, but not on a competitive level. When my dad started his bike shop, it was a business; he was an enthusiast making a living for his family. For me, well, there was a mechanic at the bike shop who was a bike racer, and so we went out riding. He said I should try racing, and so he got me into my first race. And although I crashed out, that was it: bike racing was in my blood, and it took off. That first year, I won the State Championships in Colorado, and my big nemesis was Davis Phinney. We both started in 1976, and we pushed each other to higher levels until, eventually, as a pro, I became his lead-out guy.

"Greg and I first met in the Junior Worlds cycling team in '78, when Eddie B. became coach of the US cycling squad. I got to know Greg at the Junior Worlds trials in Colorado Springs. He was certainly

1987 Tour de France: stage 18
Ron Kiefel climbs Mont Ventoux in the time trial from Carpentras to the summit.

the favorite, but I won the time trials. I was just this Colorado kid who popped up and made the Junior Worlds team. Eddie B. took the American program and he made a system. He had his camps and guys doing intervals—a very strong Eastern European regimen—but it was a system. Prior to that, we had no system at all. He made us more focused and professional. Certainly, the way he trained us made us strong for amateur racing. By the time of the 1984 Olympics, having all those Americans in the top ten was amazing [there were four in total: Alexi Grewal, who won gold; Davis Phinney, fifth; Thurlow Rogers, sixth; and Ron, ninth].

"Greg is really honest. He just goes out there and starts talking. If you've ever been in an autograph line with Greg, it takes four times as long as it should."

"Greg left in 1981 to do his own European thing, and that's when the split happened. Greg was an amazing diamond in the rough: he'd go out and eat McDonald's, play and party, but he'd also train super hard and recover much quicker than any of us could—that was his genetic gift. That 'gift' helped us get a bronze medal in '78 at the Junior Worlds in Washington, DC, and it happened mostly because we had Greg LeMond in our team. We all pulled hard, but Greg would go to the front and do these monster pulls. He'd take us up to speed and hold us there. We'd be challenged to keep it there, and instead of doing a thirty-second pull like Greg did, we'd do fifteen seconds. Greg would get out there and we'd hit some rollers, but he'd maintain that speed. He was so smooth and steady, and he'd hang on. You did your pull and got back and recovered . . . When the chips were down, that's when you'd see Greg's real ability.

"In the team time trial you don't just need strong guys, you need strong, smart guys. All those years of preparation doing the team time trials as an amateur, you learned a lot about yourself: how hard you should pull, what effort you should put in, how quickly you recover. You learn how to minimize your movements within the echelon and conserve your energy, dropping far back and accelerating . . . All those little things we picked up through team time trials, they all really translated well to our early years. It's a physical game, but it's also a big mental game.

"I got a phone call after the 1984 Olympics from Jim Ochowicz, who said, 'Ron, what are you thinking about for next year?' My mom wanted me to finish school, but Jim said, 'Do you really want to go to the Seoul Olympics in '88? We're starting a pro team—what do you think?' And then we went and had a training camp and trained hard, and out of that we got an invitation to race in the Giro d'Italia [of 1985]. The first week was hell for a time, but Davis [Phinney] was in there in the sprints getting sixth and seventh, and Andy Hampsten and I hung out. I won stage 15 in Perugia and Andy won stage 17, and that cemented the Americans in 1980s European cycling.

"When we came over in '85, we didn't know what we didn't know. We didn't know all the European history—at least I didn't—and so we were pretty independent and [did our own thing]. We brought in Shelley Verses [professional cycling's first female soigneur] and we'd go out and walk around or eat ice cream or laugh at the dinner table. We'd have a lot of fun. But those other team tables . . . Those guys were serious and stoic, and so when people like Sean Yates [at that time with Peugeot] came over to talk to us, they were drawn to our team because, shit, we were havin' fun! Bike racing was hard, but we were laughing at ourselves, celebrating our successes. We'd be drinking and laughing and having a good time. We'd be pissed if we didn't win, but we'd tell some stories and it'd be like, 'We didn't die—we'll get up the next day and go for it.' I think that attitude was very refreshing to the Europeans; those European sporting directors are no fun. They ruled with an iron fist.

"When I turned pro, one of my first races was at the Tour Méditerranéen. I was bumping handlebars with this little guy right next to me, and Dag Otto Lauritzen behind me shouts, 'Hey Ron, you know who that is?' And I say, 'No, who is that little French squirt?' [and Lauritzen replies,] 'Oh, that's Bernard Hinault!' I didn't know who any of those guys were, so I wasn't really that intimidated. I knew the racing was hard: the first hour was a piece of cake, but the last two hours were . . . holy cow! It was relaxed at the beginning, but when the TV helicopter or some sporting director came out . . . bam! The hammer dropped and it was harder and faster than anything I had done before as an amateur. That's when you got that sense of respect.

"We were always supportive of Greg, so he wasn't pissed off when we came over to Europe [too]. When we turned pro, we had a lot of respect for what he'd done. And in 1985 we went out and trained in Rancho Murieta with him. We were serious in training, and half the time Greg'd say he'd show up, but he'd go play golf instead. But Greg was serious in his own way. We came out really blazing, and it took Greg a while to get back into shape.

"Greg is really honest. He just goes out there and starts talking. If you've ever been in an autograph line with Greg, it takes four times as long as it should. Throughout our racing career, I never had a sense he was deceptive—unlike the Belgian guys . . . But not Greg. He always thought a little bit outside the box, and that's what made him that revolutionary guy: he didn't have a tradition that weighed him down.

"For anybody that makes the Tour de France and is 'in the battle' . . . I have great respect for all those guys: I know the effort and tenacity it takes."

"In 1989, at the Tour de Trump, we at 7-Eleven knew about the triathlon handlebars, but we were trying to keep them in reserve for the Tour de France. However, things changed. Dag Otto Lauritzen had started the race with a three minute lead, but every day kept losing twenty seconds, thirty seconds, to Eric Vanderaerden, the Belgian sprinter, at all these different finishes. And so Dag Otto begged the team to use the tri-bars. It was really Andy Hampsten's decision, as he wanted to keep them as a secret weapon for the Tour de France, but he relented and so we got them out—we'd done a little training with them. I remember being on the start ramp, the boardwalk in New Jersey. Sean Yates [by then with 7-Eleven] went flashing by and took the lead by fifty-five seconds, and I knew what I had to do: I rode really hard and won the stage. More importantly, though, we realized that those handlebars really did make a difference. At the Tour de France, LeMond was fortunate in that he was racing against an arrogant French guy. Fignon had to have his ponytail flapping; he had to have that 'look.' LeMond was like, 'I'm gonna frickin' . . .'

"For the Tour de France, I didn't know either the stories or the culture. In my first year as a pro, I should have been afraid . . . I remember five days before the end of the Tour, I told myself, 'If I can make it to Paris, I'll never have to ride this goddamn race again.' I made that promise, but thereafter I forgot about it. That attitude really came from our early racing in Europe, going over with Eddie B. and the national team. I know that Davis [Phinney] and myself and Andy Hampsten—we were the core group of guys. I remember we did a race in Italy in April, and it rained and it was cold; we'd go through the mountains and it'd be seven or ten degrees. Davis and I were the only two guys left from the national team. Davis almost won in a downpour, but he couldn't get his heavy plastic raincoat off. So there he was, sprinting in this big plastic raincoat, and he gets nipped right at the line. We carried that 'you just don't quit' [maxim]. Sometimes, it's not about winning, it's about finishing. By the time you get to turning pro, everybody's been known to be that tenacious person. You think about not quitting, but also how you can have an impact on the race.

"In 1986, in the mid-part of the Tour de France, I remember that Greg was just so frustrated with Hinault and all of that. For me, it was like, 'Greg, let us know how we can help.' I certainly wanted to see him win the Tour that year. When we showed up, he was pretty upset that this American team had all the attention, whereas it had been on him, as the prodigy. Between 1980 and 1984, we had a lot of success in the US press. Greg was in Europe, suffering: he was a big deal there, but not so well known in America. Myself and Davis and Andy were the big stars because of our Coors Classic and all that. But by 1986 in Europe, we were just a sideshow [to Greg]. He wanted to win, he wanted that support, but he earned it. He put in the time.

"Greg was a friend so we would talk and have fun. But when it came time to go and do his thing, he was up there and going. For me, Greg had always been on a pedestal. He had that physical advantage . . . We went to Mexico once. Greg flies down there and forgets his shoes so he uses Phinney's shoes. He stuffs some paper in the front and goes up and wins the first race! This was in the early 1980s—maybe '79, or '80. Jeff Bradley was the king of junior bike racing until Greg showed up. Those two struck up a really good friendship. Greg was a phenomenal talent, and he had a really serious side to him, but he did have a lot of fun. Jeff and Greg got into all sorts of trouble all the time. I was party to some of that, but those two, man . . . They just brushed it off and rode hard. Greg could keep going, but Jeff couldn't hang on as long as Greg could. We'd go out and drink and go dancing and raise some hell. Greg's always had so much energy, but he could do all that and come back and win the race the next day while the rest of us would suffer. As everyone else started getting weaker, he stayed at the same level and could take the pain. He always seemed to be able to last a little longer than anyone else.

"For anybody that makes the Tour and is 'in the battle' . . . I have great respect for all those guys: I know the effort and tenacity it takes. And I mean the whole collective group. You have the guys that can win stages, which is another level up, and then you have the guys that can win the race and then win it several times. If he hadn't been shot, Greg would have won more times; he was a better rider [than Stephen Roche or Pedro Delgado]. For someone to be 'the man,' they have to be incredibly tenacious. When the chips are down, they stay in

there—even if they're feeling crappy. I remember one day on the '86 Tour when Greg had terrible stomach problems. He'd just shit himself, but he stuck in the group. He was really uncomfortable and stinky and gross, but he knew exactly what he had to do to survive it.

"Greg was too nice sometimes. That's where the other guys could try to influence him . . . In the early years, it got used against him, but later on he wised up to that."

"Greg was sharp, too; he was smart. He had a good sense of the competition and other riders and was real astute, although sometimes this didn't come across. Greg was too nice sometimes. That's where the other guys could try to influence him . . . In the early years, it got used against him, but later on he wised up to that. In '89, '90, he wasn't gonna listen to any of that. There's no doubt Greg winning meant he brought the Tour de France to America."

1990 Tour de Trump
Greg and Ron pose for the cameras on the starting line.

84

Team: Renault-Elf-Gitane

2nd: Tiel (post-Tour criterium, Netherlands)

3rd: Critérium du Dauphiné Libéré
1st: stage 7b
3rd: stage 5

3rd: Emmen (post-Tour criterium, Netherlands)

3rd: Kampen (post-Tour criterium, Netherlands)

3rd: Liège-Bastogne-Liège

3rd: Tour de France
1st: young rider competition (white jersey)
3rd: stage 18
4th: stage 22
6th: stage 17
8th: stages 15 and 19
9th: prologue and stage 1
10th: stage 7

5th: Tirreno-Adriatico
2nd: stage 6
3rd: stage 3
4th: stages 4 and 5

5th: Woerden (post-Tour criterium, Netherlands)

7th: Tour of Holland
3rd: stage 5

8th: Critérium International
2nd: la course en ligne
8th: time trial

9th: Gent–Wevelgem

15th: Tour of Flanders

21st: Tour of Luxembourg

27th: UCI Road World Championships (Barcelona, Spain)

30th: La Flèche Wallonne

Tour de France
Laurent Fignon and the rest of the 1984 Renault Tour de France team are presented to the public at the Hôtel de Ville in Paris.

"One rider would work for me on certain races, as my domestique, and then I'd work for him as his domestique in other races. That's probably why we [the Renault team], individually, had fewer victories, because we rode as a team. If Charly Mottet was going well, we all worked for him; or if Laurent Fignon was doing very well at the Critérium International, we all worked for him. This was a huge change and different way of racing at the start of the '80s, so then everyone . . . most teams [began working] that way. They had to."

Greg LeMond

83
25
42

OPPOSITE **Tour of Flanders**
Greg was criticized in some quarters for not riding "everything" as reigning World Champion. Eddy Merckx, for example, said that a rider in the World Champion's jersey should ride every race as if to win it. But the world of cycling was changing, and such an approach to racing wasn't always possible. Needless to say, the two Tour winners eventually resolved their differences (on a live Belgian TV talk show). In 1984, however, Greg could hardly be criticized for not racing to win: he finished fifteenth at the Tour of Flanders that year, a week before riding Paris–Roubaix.

ABOVE **Gent-Wevelgem**
"I loved the cobbles. I came to Belgium when I was sixteen, in August of 1978, and every race we selected we looked for a race with the 'stones. I came back the year after, too, in '79, and spent six weeks by myself living with a family. I stayed in Aalst, which is not far from the hills. Every day I would seek out sections of cobblestones to ride, and I raced any race that had cobblestones. I wanted to, because I loved them."
Greg LeMond

Paris–Roubaix
Minutes before this photo was taken, the barriers had closed to allow a freight train to pass, separating the leaders from a big group of favorites chasing behind (Greg, wearing no. 24, included). The train, however, had come to a halt just before the grade crossing to allow the race to continue. Such is the importance of this classic event.

2
MERLIN
51
123
63
MERLIN

Paris–Roubaix
In the dry it's the dust that eats into your lungs, and in the wet it's the mud that gets in your eyes. Either way, the elements don't help much in the race they call "L'Enfer du Nord" (The Hell of the North).

Paris-Roubaix
The early cobbled sections of Paris-Roubaix are undulating and set into valleys, so they drain well when it rains and stay fairly dry. In 1984, however, there was plenty of mud later in the race.

Tour de France: stage 18
Riders navigate the Col du Galibier on their way to La Plagne. The 1984 Tour marks a watershed in the history of the Renault team. Despite morale being high, the team was about to split and make way for a new "superteam": La Vie Claire. Renault also lost its sponsor, and Cyrille Guimard had to start again.

SKIL
Reydel
sem
MAVIC
SKIL
Reydel
10
51

"Guimard recruited me at eighteen years old. The same year, he recruited Marc Madiot. Then he recruited Laurent Fignon a year later, and then Charly Mottet. We won ten stages on the '84 Tour de France, and were first and third overall."

Greg LeMond

ABOVE, TOP
Tour de France: stage 11
"At the '84 Tour I was sick; that was the biggest setback psychologically. I was on antibiotics for two weeks, and I was so sick. Most riders would have quit."
Greg LeMond

ABOVE **Tour de France**
Greg recovers after a crash in the Pyrenees. Despite illness and bad luck, he would go on to win the white jersey and finish third overall in Paris.

MERLIN
PLAGE
EQUIPE
Super
Croix

Tapie and the $1,000,000 contract

"In 1984, some woman came up to me on a motorcycle and said that Bernard Tapie wanted to work with me. I knew that Tapie wanted to reinforce his team in 1984. So, this black-leathered woman takes her helmet off and walks toward me. 'Monsieur LeMond?' she asks. 'Yeah?' I reply. 'Monsieur Tapie would like to see you,' she says. 'Come with me.'

"I don't even remember thinking what it was about. I got on the motorcycle, holding on to the woman's waist, and we went off to this hideout. This was going to be about being a co-leader with Hinault. When I got there, I opened the door and Tapie was holding up a Look pedal. His first words were: 'How would you like to make more money than you have ever imagined in cycling?' And he holds up this pedal, saying, 'This pedal is going to change cycling,' and that he wanted me, that I was the next Hinault. 'I'll pay you one dollar a pedal,' he says. I've still got the contract in my office downstairs. He offered me a million dollars over three years. I went back to my room—my head was spinning.

"I couldn't sleep that night. You think you've maximized your earning capacity [but you haven't]. Obviously, Guimard had heard rumors, and he needed to up my salary. I remember him saying that he understood I'd had an offer, but it wasn't about the money, it was about the Tour de France, and only after I'd won it four or five times—then the money would come. I asked him for $60,000 more and he said no. I was on antibiotics that year, and he said, 'Greg, you're the biggest talent I ever had. You did the Tour on one leg this year. But without me, you're not going to win the Tour de France.' I wondered: is he doping? But no—I think he thought it was due to strategy. Maybe he was implying I would be the leader and Fignon wouldn't be."

Greg LeMond

Tour de France: stage 20

"Guimard changed cycling in the way he built a superteam. At that time, coming in from the '60s and '70s, the team was built around Eddy Merckx. Merckx was the boss, and every race he entered everybody raced for Merckx, so it didn't matter how good they were or how bad he was. Guimard felt it was too risky to place the pressure on one rider for the whole season, especially when the budgets at that time were getting bigger and bigger."

Greg LeMond

ABOVE, TOP
Tour de France: stage 21
Despite teammate Vincent Barteau's playful interference, Laurent Fignon, the team leader, would eventually win the stage. He had more than ten minutes to spare by the time the riders got to Paris.

ABOVE **Post-Tour party at the Soirée a l'Alcazar, Paris**
Guimard and members of the victorious Renault team celebrate their success. Barteau (in the bejewelled G-string) appears to be having a particularly good time.

"Do what you want. Say what you want. I ain't going home."

STEPHEN ROCHE

PREVIOUS SPREAD
"The Tour of Flanders and Paris–Roubaix: that week in April is just magical."
Greg LeMond

ABOVE **Tour de France**
Stephen Roche and Greg seemed happier rivals than Bernard Hinault and Greg. Hinault, for example, would never mess about for the cameras.

The Enemy Within

For Irishman Stephen Roche, 1985 was a turning point. He'd already been recognized as a major talent, and both he and Greg had been tipped as potential winners of the Tour de France. That year, however, Roche unwittingly became the architect of a rift at the top of the Tour's leader board. On stage 17, Roche took his chance and, with Pedro Delgado and Fabio Parra, attacked the leaders and built up a gap. That climbers of their caliber should escape was no great surprise, but with Roche sitting in third place overall, second-placed Greg LeMond decided to go with them. The notable absentee from this group was Bernard Hinault, the yellow jersey holder and Greg's teammate, who was left struggling behind. The resulting breakaway stalemate began one of the biggest rivalries in cycling history.

Roche was an effortless, almost lackadaisical pedalist, a rider with the style of a dancer—*a la danseuse*, as the French would say. He rarely made a mistake, and was able to mask his difficulties like no one else (in cycling, bluff is sometimes all you have). As his career progressed, he'd have to call on this talent, too. Cycling is not a sport for the faint-hearted, and despite the suffering that goes on in the mountains, very often it's your rivals and adversaries that create the most danger and anxiety. When those rivals are your teammates, cycling can reveal one of its darkest, most treacherous sides. If Greg's nemesis in 1985 was Bernard Hinault, then Roche's in 1987 would undoubtedly be the Italian Roberto Visentini. As teammates with very similar ambitions, their rivalry came to a spectacular head-to-head during the 1987 Giro d'Italia.

Roche's career was cemented by his incredible treble, winning cycling's Triple Crown in 1987 and joining Eddy Merckx as one of only two riders in the history of the sport to win the Tour de France, the Giro d'Italia, and the World Championships in the same year. Many great riders are ultimately thwarted by a serious injury, forcing them to spend the rest of their careers defending or guarding their position. For Roche, it would be a knee injury caused by an accident on the track during a six-day event in 1986. The problems it created were only exacerbated by a relentless racing schedule and pressure to perform in every race. Roche's injured knee would be his Achilles' heel, preventing any reprise of his great performances of 1987.

Prior to the Tour in '85, Stephen and Greg had fairly similar race programs, and despite having youth and enthusiasm on their side, they were often overtrained, under-rested, and in many ways physically abused by their teams and managers. Indeed, Roche was once told by his directeur sportif that he'd be "sent home to Ireland" if he didn't win the Paris–Roubaix Espoirs (he did).

Both Stephen and Greg were exceptionally talented all-rounders and Grand Tour specialists, with a variety of unique talents at their disposal: Greg could sprint and descend with the best of them, whereas Stephen was a strong climber and an excellent time trialist. What's more, neither seemed to have a particular weakness. So, if it hadn't been for their respective injuries, they would no doubt have produced many more mouthwatering duels.

In 1985, bike racing appeared to change for a variety of reasons. Not least among them, perhaps, was the fact that English-speaking riders were starting to make a difference to the results. They were starting to take over.

1990 Paris–Nice
After a series of post-Triple Crown seasons dogged by injury, Stephen Roche looks to return to racing.

1985:
Stephen Roche

"Three days before [stage 17 of the 1985 Tour de France], Hinault, in the yellow jersey, had fallen at Saint-Étienne. Everyone was speculating [whether] he had a broken nose. He wore these dark shades that hid his black eye, so we couldn't really tell [whether the stories were genuine or not], but I think he got away with it. Myself, Greg, and Pedro Delgado got away [from the pack], and then we were riding for a time with Hinault behind. We'd started on the Col d'Aspin, then rode the Col du Tourmalet, and finished on Luz Ardiden. So we started the final climb, and we were getting time checks from Greg's car [on Hinault's position], around the one and a half, two minute mark. That day on the climb up to Luz Ardiden, Greg wouldn't ride with me, but he kept attacking me, so I kept riding at 80 percent because I knew I was third or fourth overall on GC [general classification]. I also knew that if Greg got away from me, I could say goodbye to winning the Tour that year. So I felt by holding on to Greg, I could hopefully do as good or better than him in the time trial. And I wasn't going to bury myself in the road and have him attack me and then get away from me altogether.

"We got caught near the top, but Hinault wasn't there."

"We got time checks from Greg's car [again], and they seemed to be okay—in and around the one and a half, two minute mark. We didn't seem to be losing any time, officially. What was actually happening was that [Paul] Koechli was lying, because he was making us feel we were comfortable whereas, in fact, Hinault was charging behind, catching up on us. If we had known Hinault was coming back at us, I'd have worked a bit harder with Greg and maybe tried to put more time into Hinault. Koechli was telling Greg that Hinault was almost two minutes back. So I thought, I don't have to worry about Hinault, I have to worry about Greg. But in fact Hinault was closing in on us all the time. I remember Greg kept trying to attack, attack, attack, but I said, 'Greg, forget about it. He ain't going nowhere.' And I knew if I rode 100 percent Greg would've attacked me and I wouldn't have been able to catch him back. So I just rode at 80 percent and matched him. We got caught near the top, but Hinault wasn't with them.

"Greg was definitely the stronger rider that year. Maybe in '86 it was the contrary, [but] definitely in '85 Greg was stronger than Hinault. Perhaps Hinault held him back. The rivalry? I didn't pay much attention to it. We weren't really aware of all the rivalry because they put on a good show—until stage 17! Greg wouldn't have won that stage alone [Delgado did], but we could have gone on and made up more time [on Hinault]. But on the Tour in general, if Greg had played his own hand, I think yes, he probably was stronger than Hinault. But we weren't aware of the hard rivalry that happened in later months.

"When the '85 Tour was announced in October '84, they announced a 55 kilometer morning stage up to Aubisque, with 100 kilometers in the afternoon on the other side of the Aubisque back into Pau. And our DS Raphaël Géminiani said, Roche is going to win those two stages. He said, he's gonna win them because he has an incredible turn of speed, and he won't only win the morning stage, he'll win the afternoon as well. That's pressure for you! He maintained that story right through the whole of the year. Right up to the morning of the stage, when he came to my room and gave me a specially commissioned skinsuit that had a silky aerodynamic top, and silk wasn't really done in those days. 'Here, Stephen,' he said. 'Here's your winning outfit for the stage.' 'I can't go on the start line with that!' I replied. 'Everyone knows. Everyone listens to you saying Roche is going to win. If I wear that, everyone will say I'm crazy!' I put a jersey on over it because I didn't want to go down to the start line in a skinsuit with no pockets or anything in it. On the Aubisque, I took my jersey off and threw it on the ground.

"At the foot of the Col du Soulor, the Colombian Lucho [Luis] Herrera had already got away. There was a fairly good gap, so the pressure was really, really on. I'd missed out on the rewards the day before, but here was another mountain stage that I could do well on, so I took off and caught Herrera. I was surprised first of all to catch him, and then I began to think, 'Has Hinault done a deal with Herrera?' Everything goes through your mind because it wasn't normal, catching Herrera. 'Is this normal?' So I attacked him straight away and held on to win the stage while Hinault was fighting it out with LeMond and Sean Kelly behind me. But it was another opportunity to put time into Hinault and LeMond, primarily because the pressure was on. There were two races there: it was the race and the race within.

"When it happened to me [Roche's battle with Roberto Visentini at the 1987 Giro d'Italia], my attitude was: do what you want, say what you want, but I ain't going home. That was my barrier; it helped me sleep at night. It didn't matter what they said, as there was no way I was going home. I'm here to win, I thought, and if I don't win, it's not because I haven't tried. It's not because you've spat at me or said something to me, it's other factors.

"My battle lasted twelve days. It had a draining effect, but I coped with it because I blocked everything out. It's very hard for the staff—the masseurs, the mechanics, the managers of the team—to keep the balance. The most difficult part for me, apart from the crowd, was the team itself. The team was unanimously for Visentini, and [I had] just one teammate riding for me [the Belgian Eddy Schepers]. It wasn't the same thing with La Vie Claire, or it wasn't visible from the outside at any rate, but I'm sure it was similar with Hinault being French and having all his French domestiques around him. I'm sure there was a lot of tension within the team as well.

"Tapie brought things to a different level: the motorhomes, the VIPs, the champagne at the finishing line. He brought a higher profile to the sport, and things have benefited greatly since that era."

"Greg was a different rider when he came back after his hunting accident. He was much more choosy in which races he rode, and prepared more for specific races. Which got him abuse in the press as well. After he won the Tour in '86, I think that's all he wanted to do—to focus on the Tour. It was always something people had difficulty coming to terms with. They said he showed a lack of respect for races, coming along and 'just' riding around. Before his injury, he rode a similar program to myself—120 days a year—and there was a different style of rider. After he had the accident and came back in '88, '89, '90, he was more cautious and mostly focused on the Tour. Which was disappointing to some because of the rider he was . . . It caused a lot of speculation as to his commitment. Hamburgers and Coca-Cola! All the remarks going round [suggested that he was eating] too much shit food and didn't care about the Dauphiné or the Romandie. It was all about the Tour.

"Injuries definitely played a big part for all of us in those days. It's difficult to say where things would have gone in my career, or Greg's, without them. People might ask, would I have won the '87 Tour if Greg had been there and Hinault hadn't retired? In '85, it was Hinault, Greg, and myself. In '86, Greg wins, but in '87 they're gone and I'm there. Would he have won if he hadn't had his accident, they might ask. I'd say no, obviously, but every event has its own little drama of ups and downs. But then if Greg hadn't had his accident, would he have won six Tours? We'll never know.

"In '85, when I won on the Aubisque, I was coming down off the finishing line and Bernard Tapie had his motorhome there. As I walked past he pulled me inside. Greg and Hinault were there, and Tapie offered me a glass of champagne. 'Don't you come round and fuck us up now!' he said to me. Then everything started moving off the climb and I had to stay in this van. All the media speculation the next day was wondering, what did Tapie say to Roche? Is he signing him for next year?'

"I'd had a few run-ins with Hinault as well, but it never got as verbal as it did between him and Greg. But Greg was on his team, so Greg got an awful lot of attention from Tapie, which Hinault was jealous about too. I know Greg got abuse from Hinault maybe more than the other English-speaking riders because his contract was highlighted a lot in the papers—Tapie giving him a million dollars for three years, or whatever it was, and Hinault wasn't getting that. The national hero, who had won the Tour four times already . . . Here was this young kid with blond hair and braces.

"Tapie brought things to a different level: the motorhomes, the VIPs, the champagne at the finishing line. He brought a higher profile to the sport, and cycling has benefited greatly since that era. Tapie saw an opportunity . . . He's a real people-person, and he saw a business opportunity in signing LeMond. Tapie was [paying] a million dollars rather than the twenty or thirty grand you'd expect at the time. That was amazing—a lot of money—but he saw the opportunity with La Vie Claire and wanted to use Greg LeMond as his marketing tool.

"When you know the danger is coming from the outside, you can manage it. But when the danger is coming from inside your own team—and it's by no means a small danger having the likes of Hinault or Visentini up against you—they're icons in their countries and as good as you on the day. You have to be very careful in everything you do. You're being overcautious on what you're eating, drinking, bike, tires, your choice of gearing . . . You hadn't a big choice of gears, but you had to have the right gears. You don't want to lose it all over a small detail. You can't leave any stone unturned; you have to get into everything. You're more into the way of thinking, what losing time means here or what gaining time means there . . .

"It does make you be on your best behavior, because it can all go wrong, very easily."

Tour de France: stage 17
Toulouse to Luz Ardiden was a frustrating day for Greg. Full of riding and strength, he could have undoubtedly gone on and made up time on his teammate Hinault. The La Vie Claire management of Paul Koechli and Bernard Tapie made sure that didn't happen.

Team: La Vie Claire-Radar

1st: Coors Classic
1st: stage 5

2nd: Tour de France
1st: stage 21
2nd: points classification (green jersey) and stage 6
3rd: stage 14
4th: stages 8 and 15
5th: prologue and stages 11 and 17
6th: stage 18b
7th: stage 18a
8th: stage 19
10th: stage 12

2nd: UCI Road World Championships (Giavera del Montello, Italy)

2nd: Vuelta al País Vasco
2nd: stages 2 and 3
3rd: stage 4b

3rd: Giro d'Italia
3rd: stage 12
4th: stage 22
5th: stages 15 and 20
6th: stages 4 and 14
7th: stage 13
8th: stages 8b and 10
9th: stage 8a

4th: Critérium International
4th: hill climb
8th: time trial

4th: Omloop Het Volk

4th: Paris-Roubaix

5th: Vuelta a Valencia
3rd: stages 3 and 4
4th: stage 1

6th: Tour Méditerranéen
4th: stage 4a

7th: Grand Prix Eddy Merckx

7th: Tour of Flanders

8th: Baracchi Trophy (with Bernard Hinault)

17th: Liège-Bastogne-Liège

18th: Gent-Wevelgem

47th: Paris-Brussels

Tirreno-Adriatico
2nd: stage 4
3rd: stage 1

Tour de France: stage 3
The team time trial from Vitre to Fougères. La Vie Claire were unstoppable.

Coors Classic
Greg with Kathy at his only win of 1985. The Coors Classic became popular with many of the best riders. The prize money was good, and with increasing TV interest in the Tour de France, it formed a big part of the season for American riders racing at home and in Europe.

Paris–Roubaix
Fourth at the 1985 Paris–Roubaix was a good result for Greg, especially given the terrible weather and the battle-hardened competition. Greg's former teammate from Renault days Marc Madiot was the eventual winner, with only thirty-five riders making it to the velodrome in Roubaix.

Paris–Roubaix
Greg's fourth place in 1985 was not only a very respectable result, it was also the first time he'd made it to the end of the race.

Paris–Roubaix
When it's wet, Paris–Roubaix turns into something very special. Together with the treacherous cobblestones, a bit of rain makes the hardest one-day bike race in the world even harder. Experienced riders will always ride in the front: following wheels is risky when the mud and water conceal deadly potholes. Greg's deft bike handling and cyclocross skills were certainly put to the test in 1985.

brancale
OAKLEY

Liège-Bastogne-Liège
Although Greg is arguably well suited to this hilly and demanding classic in the Belgian Ardennes, he was often dogged by bad luck. In 1984, he finished third; in 1985, this puncture meant he finished seventeenth.

ABOVE, TOP **Gent-Wevelgem**
"In the classics, the important thing isn't so much being the strongest rider as knowing the race itself. It took me a good three years of racing to learn how to race the classics."
Greg LeMond

ABOVE **Omloop Het Volk**
A creditable fourth place in Het Volk and seventh at the Tour of Flanders were great results for Greg, underlining his abilities on the cobbles. He was getting noticed by the Belgian fans, and was gaining major support in his new homeland.

“In Europe, the only thing that was hard was the weather, the homesickness, not speaking the language and catching colds—all of that.”

Greg LeMond

In 1985, the bikes ridden at the Tour de France were pretty much the same as they'd been twenty years earlier. In the next decade or so, bicycle technology was about to take a huge leap forward.

Giro d'Italia: stage 20
In 1985, Bernard Hinault and La Vie Claire dominated the Giro d'Italia, with Hinault set to win two Grand Tours in one year. Greg finished third, and both riders carried their form forward to the Tour de France. Stage 20 of the '85 Giro, from St. Vincent d'Aosta to Valnontey Gran Paradiso, was won by Andy Hampsten.

Tour de France: stage 15

"In a way, Hinault should not have won that Tour. It doesn't matter if he's the strongest in the first week; that doesn't make a difference. It's who's the strongest over three weeks. But I wasn't mad at Hinault. I wasn't pissed at him at all. Hinault wasn't telling [the team] what to do. It was Bernard Tapie's and Paul Koechli's conspiracy to make sure Hinault won his fifth Tour. I had nothing against Hinault—I wanted him to win the Tour—but if Hinault had been in my place on Luz Ardiden, he would not have waited."

Greg LeMond

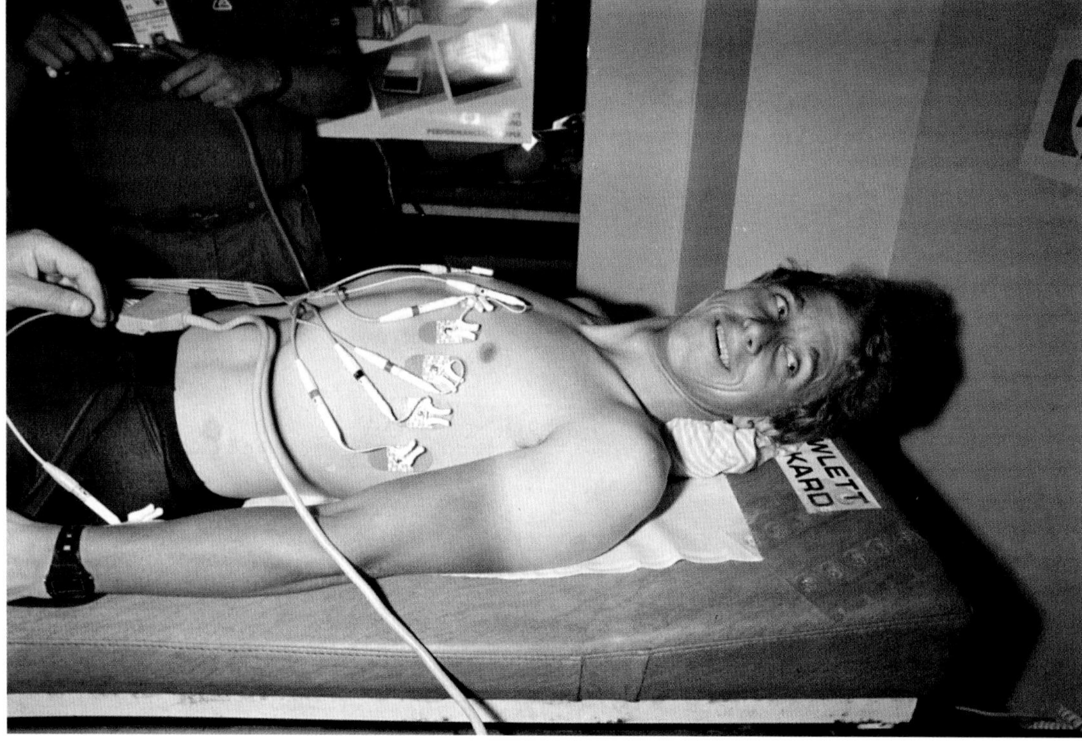

ABOVE, TOP
"I was so nervous about the 1985 Tour. I was racing conservatively, but physically '85 and '86 were a breeze."
Greg LeMond

ABOVE **Tour de France**
All the riders went through health checks before the start of a Tour. It was a relaxed start to a race that, in 1985, would shape Greg's career and change his attitude toward winning the world's biggest bike race.

ABOVE, TOP

Tour de France: stage 7

This was a summer outing on the roads of Paris-Roubaix. The stage finished in Roubaix, the regular finishing point of the French spring classic, and Greg used his ability and experience over the cobbles to finish a creditable thirteenth place. Many of the climbers and less experienced riders, however, had a bad day.

ABOVE

Tour de France: stage 12

Riding with Fabio Parra. On the mountainous stages, the Colombian—like many of the climbers at the 1985 Tour—took advantage of the stalemate between Hinault and Greg, winning stage 12 and riding well in his first Tour. He finished eighth overall, and won the white jersey for best young rider.

Tour de France: stage 3
A 73 kilometer team time trial from Vitré to Fougères. La Vie Claire won it convincingly from their main rivals, and placed their best riders (Hinault, Steve Bauer, and Greg) and the rest of the team in or around the top ten on general classification.

cinelli
radar
Wonder

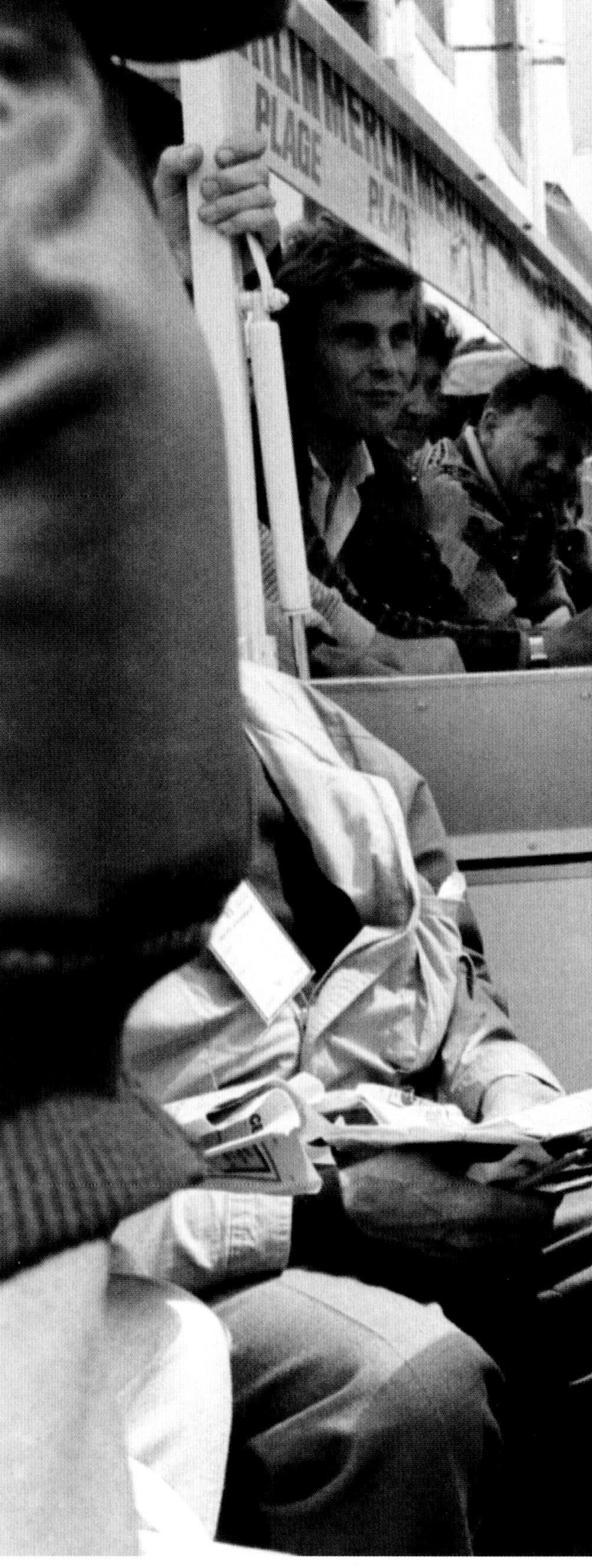

Tour de France: stage 8
The moment the '85 Tour began to slip away from Greg was the time trial in the Vosges on stage 8. Afterwards, Hinault was typically bullish, saying, "I said I was the strongest and I am proving it. The most important thing being: to prove what you claim." This was one of the longest individual time trials in Tour history. Greg managed fourth, but lost an astonishing 2 minutes 34 seconds in 75 kilometers to the Badger.

28
CREDIT LYONNAIS
HUFFY
OAKLEY
radar
Santini
HUFFY

La Vie Claire
LEMOND
La Redoute

La Vie Claire
MOND

La Vie Claire
MOND

Tour de France: stage 8
After the first uphill section of the stage, many riders changed from a climbing bike to a heavier, disc-wheeled low-profile machine for the long downhill section and fast, flat finish. Some late rain played its part in the results for a few of the key riders, but it didn't stop Hinault. He rode the same bike from start to finish, smashing the field and winning by more than two and a half minutes. Later, Greg would win the time trial at Lac Vassivière, beating Hinault and recording the first victory for an American at the Tour de France.

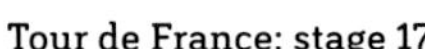

Tour de France: stage 17

"Paul Koechli [via Maurice Le Guilloux, who was in the team car behind the breakaway that day] told me, 'You cannot ride with Roche, Hinault's coming up. You need to wait for him. We want to ensure our first and second place.' We started arguing, me saying, 'Well, how far back is he?' But he wouldn't tell me, and then eventually he said, 'Forty or forty-five seconds.' As we're arguing, Luis Herrera rides off up the road [Pedro Delgado, already away, won the stage and Herrera came in second]. We kept arguing and finally I decided, okay, I'll wait. Stephen Roche had been sitting there, listening to the entire thing, and our breakaway lost its momentum. A group of about sixteen or eighteen riders comes up, and Hinault's not there. He was still another minute and a half behind that group. By the finish, he was a minute and fifteen seconds down, and I'd waited minutes for him! It wasn't until that big group came to me that I realized Hinault wasn't there, and that he was even farther down the climb behind the grupetto."

Greg LeMond

Tour de France
Stage 17 was a pivotal moment for everyone involved. No deals could be done, however, no matter how hard Greg tried.

“Hinault could win anything he wanted to, and you had to respect that. He also had a more egalitarian attitude, in that he treated everyone equally. Except for at the Tour, where he was a leader.”

Greg LeMond

Tour de France: podium presentation, Paris
"I had a very difficult time with [the spat with Hinault], because it was massively confusing for me—Hinault was my hero. I still have a lot of respect for him because, as an athlete, he was one of the best. He was an equal to Eddy Merckx. Maybe not as consumed with cycling as Merckx, but physically he was his equal."
Greg LeMond

RYOBI
7
La Vie Claire
wonder
radar LOOK
BANANIA
7
CREDIT

"If there are two meals left and a gun and the three of us—Greg, me, and Hinault—who am I going to shoot? Well, I'd shoot Hinault, obviously, because otherwise he'd shoot me and Greg and eat both the meals."

ROBERT MILLAR

PREVIOUS SPREAD
Tour de France: stage 21
Greg faces the press in Saint-Étienne before the penultimate stage to the Puy-de-Dôme.

ABOVE **1984 Tour de France**
Robert Millar, with Laurent Fignon and Greg behind. The Scot would finish the Tour eight times in his career, with three stage victories. In 1984, Millar won stage 11 and the polka-dot jersey in the mountains classification.

The Scot, the Breton, and the American

Another English-speaking rider from outside the Eurocentric closed shop of 1980s cycling was the Scot Robert Millar. His fourth place at the 1984 Tour de France announced him as a young, gifted leader for French team Peugeot, and he was the first rider from an English-speaking nation to win the polka-dot 'King of the Mountains' jersey for best climber. Suffice it to say that if he'd been racing in the modern era with the support of a team built around these talents, his palmares would have looked a lot different. But his climbing ability was extraordinary, and he was seen as the first British rider with the potential to win the Tour de France outright. His journey to the Tour was far from an easy ride. For Millar, in the early '80s, it meant being thrown into the French cycling world as a junior at ACBB, the Paris amateur club with direct links to the Peugeot professional team. He, like many of his peers, then had to fight for his place.

Millar always let his legs do the talking. Never a rider for excuses, his quiet, direct manner meant he was regarded by some in the media as taciturn and difficult off the bike, but his riding abilities only proved that he was canny and clever on it. As a result, he became a popular choice among teams looking for a solid GC rider who could ride well in any situation, especially in stage races with mountains, notably winning the Volta a Catalunya in 1985 and the Critérium du Dauphiné Libéré in 1990. He came close to winning the Vuelta a España in 1985, with only some collusion and skulduggery on behalf of the home teams dropping him into second place on the penultimate stage after a puncture. He finished second again in 1986, and was runner-up at the 1987 Giro d'Italia. He rode the Tour eleven times, and although he never won the race outright, he came first in three stages and always rose up the general classification when the race hit the hills.

As if to underline his racing pedigree, Millar became a consistent finisher at the World Championships too, in an era when the British team was distinctly lacking in support for a rider of Millar's caliber. Regular top ten finishes in such races as Liège–Bastogne–Liège, La Flèche Wallonne, and the Tour of Lombardy proved he could handle the hilliest and toughest of the one day classics. At the Grand Tours, Millar's climbing ability and willingness to help out was often relied on by isolated English-speaking riders finding themselves in a bit of trouble, such as Stephen Roche at the 1987 Giro d'Italia, Sean Kelly at the 1988 Vuelta a España, and, most poignantly, Greg LeMond at the 1986 and 1989 Tours de France.

Millar's outlook on the world of professional cycling has always been a mixture of cynical realism and passionate enthusiasm. Since his retirement from racing in 1993, he has written concisely and perceptively about the sport for magazines and the Internet. He can explain a racing situation like no other writer, mostly because he's been there, but also because he has a calm and insightful intelligence.

When naming their best climbers, or their "road racer's road racer," Robert Millar's name is often at the top of many cycling fans' lists. Millar's talent meant that, when Greg joined forces with him on team Z in 1990, the American found himself riding for an outfit that could handle the hills. Although the two riders were polar opposites in terms of character, they had a mutual respect and regularly worked as allies against the rest—even, as in 1989, when on opposing teams. With their attacking riding styles and natural climbing abilities, they often found themselves together at the sharp end of some of the hardest races and stages at cycling's biggest events. In 1986 at the Tour de France, however, Millar, riding for the Panasonic team, took a backseat as Hinault and Greg fought their final duel.

1986:
Robert Millar

"You just watched [Greg and Hinault] squabbling. When you're in that situation, naturally you take sides, and it's the one you hate the least that you side with because you're meant to be competing with them. You couldn't really like Hinault as a competitor, and Greg has that kind of character where you just like him anyway, even if he's beating you. He was friendly. You knew that Greg would pounce on you when you were at your weakest, although at least he wouldn't provoke that moment. Greg also raised the stakes because everybody's wages went up, although that meant that the team managers started to put pressure on you and the races became more and more important. So you had to put aside any friendships and get on with what you were doing.

"Greg could really beat the crap out of you, if he wanted to. You didn't want to ride with him, because you knew he was going to beat you."

"At first, you didn't mind Greg doing well, because he was clearly very talented and it was good for everybody. But once the team managers started to put pressure on you and the dynamics of your friendships with all the other guys changed . . . If you had to make a choice between Hinault and Greg, you chose Greg, but your team manager still wanted you to beat him, regardless of alliances. And that was quite difficult because the guy's better than you. He's physically better than you, so, as a rider, you're looking for a weakness or terrains where you can be at least as competitive as him—and there aren't many of those. For me, the only time I could beat Greg was uphill. In his early career, his climbing wasn't as good, but everything else was slightly better. But as he lost weight, his climbing improved. Like all cyclists, though, that took an edge off his sprinting and time trialing.

"We all had different talents, but it put more pressure on the team leaders to win. It was strange to see, because the dynamics changed for all of us. I was at the Panasonic team [in 1986]. I was still being sent to two big tours, and I just didn't want to do that. I would have rather ridden for the mountains classifications and been the best climber. I always wanted to be a great climber, rather than a second-rate GC rider who 'just' finished in the top ten; that didn't matter to me. When I first turned professional, in 1980, you didn't speak English. There were maybe a couple of guys who did, but you just didn't speak it. You spoke French otherwise you just didn't fit in, and you wouldn't have lasted long enough. But there was Phil Anderson, Sean Yates, and myself. Sean Kelly was already there and was best 'foreigner,' then Roche and LeMond appeared in 1981.

"In 1982, I finished second at the Tour de l'Avenir. Greg was just better than me everywhere. I didn't really race against him; I was just the first of the other guys he beat. He won by ten minutes. He was just so far in front in most of the disciplines that we were just racing for second place. I remember we went up Mont Ventoux, and there were only three of us left in the front. We attacked Greg all the way up Ventoux, and he just rode at the same level we could. I realized then that Greg was just getting better and better. I mean, normally on a major climb on that type of terrain, we'd have blown him out, but we didn't. We couldn't.

"Panasonic didn't like Hinault that much, so there were a couple of times during the 1986 Tour de France when Greg was isolated and Panasonic did a deal to ride not *for* him, but not against him either, so that they had favors stored up for later. Then, in '89, when Greg had no teammates left with him in the mountains, [team Z manager Roger] Legeay told me to ride tempo sometimes, to calm things down when Fignon was attacking. Legeay was in negotiations with Greg to come to team Z in 1990, as it was announced soon after the Tour.

"Greg could really beat the crap out of you, if he wanted to. You didn't want to ride with him, because you knew he was going to beat you. In a breakaway group of five, very often people would stop riding just because Greg was there, because you knew he'd win the sprint. Unless Kelly was there, and then even Kelly might not beat him. And that situation happened quite a lot in Greg's career. It wasn't a case of Greg 'sitting on' and waiting for the time trial; it was often the way tactics would be. It's an important part of being a professional cyclist: if it's not working out in the breakaway, you ride at, say, 40 percent. Then, if Greg has to lead and ride at his 60 percent, he'll eventually sit up too. Then the group behind would catch on, and you'd see what the options were—see who's there and see what happens. And then if he still wins, then fair enough. That would happen a lot. But usually he'd beat you in the sprint and in the time trial as well!

"When you come across guys who are that talented, there's not a lot to play with. They're better than you; their 100 percent is better than yours. What was really interesting about Greg was that he could be aggressive and attacking during a race, ruthlessly exploiting any weakness in his rivals, but be completely different once the race had finished. Most of the others continued to be assholes. He was best described as the least macho. Most of the time during my career, I raced against Greg, but he was never shitty. We would talk and laugh in our little group of 'foreigners.' It wasn't the atmosphere that exists nowadays. Back then, foreigners in teams were tolerated only if they could do a better job than the equivalent home rider, but for less.

"When you're young, you're all, 'Great, I'm hurting!' You're actually happy about it."

"You have a speed in your head where you get scared—a point where you're comfortable, and then one just beyond where you get scared. Everybody has that. If you're not scared, then there's something wrong with you. You go beyond comfortable and you're into the scared zone, and that happens quite a lot in racing. You're never ever comfortable there—unless you're crazy, that is. Those riders, like Greg, who were ridiculously talented going downhill, you know that they're never scared. So to stay with him was hard. He would push to try and drop you until he was feeling uncomfortable, and then I was already into the scared zone. Most descents with Greg would be okay, but the really fast ones would be horrible. You'd go into a corner, a fast one—not a hairpin, where falling off is no big deal, but one of the really big, fast, open sweepers, where you think about touching the brakes but don't dare. Those would be the worst, because he'd probably pedal into them and be leaning off the side of the bike . . . So you come out of the corner twenty meters behind, and then you'd have to close that and have to do a full sprint to get back. If you did a ten kilometer descent like that, where it was all really fast, open corners, by the time you got down, you'd be frazzled. Physically you might be okay, but mentally you'd be frazzled. Greg'd get to the bottom and be recovered, but you might never recover. You've been into the red on the way up, and on the descent you've stayed there—because you're scared.

"I had to learn to be a better descender, using relaxation techniques and such, just to stay in the front group and not be hanging on at the back. We worked hard at every aspect of racing. People presume that you just turn up and you're a good climber, so . . . But you have a certain amount of natural talent, and it's up to you to hone that to its absolute maximum. And then you look at where you are and compare it to the skills that you need. You have to choose the ones to improve.

"Nowadays, riders get to choose their programs to suit their talents, and they'll maybe do sixty-five races a year, whereas I would have done sixty-five races before the Tour de France. In those days, the team would be less specialized, so you'd have to go to the early one-day races even if you were a stage-race rider. You were sent to the one-day races to help the other guys out—ride in the front, chase down breaks, go back for bottles and jerseys, all that shit—and these races wore you out. You never really got any time off. And in the smaller races, if you weren't the team leader, you were expected to work. You had a totally different set of demands on you. In the Tour of Flanders, say, where your job would be to move the team leaders into position for the hills, you knew there was going to be a crash, and you knew that you could easily be in it . . . but you'd do it anyway. Every race, there'd be some moment when there'd be a screech of brakes and a crumple of bodies, and you'd think, I'm going to be in that. It's not normal.

"Greg got sent to all the races too, in his first years, but then you have the ability to absorb that workload. With all that time in the wind, the enthusiasm only lasts about two years, but you do it because you still can. You use that freshness for races that you want to do, like the Tour of Lombardy. You're looking at the hills, thinking, 'Oh, it'd be good to do that. All the great riders have done it, and I want to do it too.' Then, five years later, you're thinking, 'Shit! The Tour of Lombardy! Oh no . . .' And you'll still be in the front because you have the talent to be in the front, but you've lost the freshness and you don't have that hurt capacity anymore: you're hurting before you've even started. When you're young, you're all, 'Great, I'm hurting!' You're actually happy about it. But eventually, the sheer number of races sucks that life out of you.

"In 1990, I got sick just after the Millau stage of the Tour. If you look at the race images, I was already underweight and worn out, and then I caught something just after that stage. Next day—I think it was to Toulouse—I felt dreadful. I was sick at the Village Départ, then I had the trots. So when the stage started, I got spat out the back at the first acceleration. They sent Bruno Cornillet back for me, but I told him to leave me, otherwise we would have both been eliminated. I stopped after about a hundred kilometers. I was already outside the time limit, and there were still another hundred kilometers to go. I left that night, and the next time I saw the guys was at the Paris celebration.

"At the 1991 Tour, I crashed and ended up in a neck brace. Legeay was really angry when I didn't recover enough to meet his plans. As if the Tour is an environment where you get R & R! I think he thought that because I was dropped most days, I was having an easy time. On the day to Morzine, Greg got dropped early, and [Gilbert] Duclos-Lassalle and a few others were told to stay with him. Then, on the way up Joux Plane, Greg caught up with me. I was dropped from the main peloton, so I rode for him from there to the bottom of the finishing climb [Greg lost seven minutes, Millar around half an hour]. I threw up at the finish as I was so worn out, but it didn't stop Legeay being shitty with me and Atle Kvasvoll, who also was walking wounded. We ought both to have gone home before we even got to the mountains. We were broken.

"At the end of 1988, I was with Fagor and I knew I was leaving. We were doing the Tour of Catalunya and it was boiling hot. The whole race was done in one long line: you had about two minutes of talking to your friends at the start, and then it was lined out for the rest of the day. It was just ridiculously fast—all in the gutter with the Once team smashing it at the front. I remember Greg was riding with the Dutch PDM team, and it wasn't going well for him. I doubt they'd have been nice to him at PDM; their mentality always seemed to be, 'win at all costs.' That was their way of riding. But in a breathing space, Greg rolls up alongside me and asks if I thought Fagor had any space on the team for him. He was in a bad way and hadn't been near the front all year. All I said was that I was leaving and I didn't know.

"The next year, Greg wins the Tour with ADR, so how pissed off would PDM have been?! It wasn't a shock to me, though. That's Greg for you: he was so naturally talented and robust, it wasn't a surprise to see him back in 1989 at the level he was at before. Sure, he'd put on a bit of weight, but his time trialing was a lot better. After Greg won the Tour in '89, Z signed him, so he joined after me. But I didn't have a problem with that: Greg was a good person to work with. He came with the World Championships jersey, and I don't know if he was joking or not, but I remember Roger Zannier [owner of team Z] saying that he didn't want him in the rainbow jersey, he wanted the team in a Z jersey. He was all about advertising his business . . . But the Worlds jersey is still really important, because in cycling there's only three races that really 'matter': the Worlds, the Tour de France, and Paris-Roubaix. For the Worlds you get the rainbow jersey, for the Tour you get the yellow jersey, and for Paris-Roubaix . . . well, you just get the brick. In cycling, those are the only things that matter. Just look at the coverage they get.

"In 1985, Hinault did Greg over. Paul Koechli saying that Greg wasn't good enough is bullshit, but he can't admit it. We all knew that it was better for the sponsor for a French guy to win, but when you get done-over in a race, the lie is often perpetuated afterwards and people start to believe it. Hinault became unpopular with the French public anyway, almost because he was so good. He had to start giving out favors to make himself look popular again, but he was just pretending. He was still vicious, especially if he didn't get what he wanted. As his competitor, at first you think he's strong, but after a while you can see weaknesses there, so you exploit them . . . You would hurt him [by making him ride harder], and then he'd say something nasty to you and so then you'd do it again, because he'd been nasty to you. When you're competitive, it's 'normal' to physically hurt the opposition, mentally too. If you could attack them on a descent and unnerve them, you wore them out and it didn't matter how. Hinault had a nastiness beyond the norms of competition, and he could be insulting and xenophobic—that kind of crap. Greg was likable, but he just didn't have the nastiness. If he'd been like any other racer, he'd have waited until Hinault had done a really big turn and was suffering, and then he would've jumped him and left him. It's a bit like, 'tell him one thing and then I'll do him over.'

"Hinault supported Greg when he turned pro, so Greg was indebted to him. And when you like somebody and you respect them, and then they do you a bad turn, they're still your friend. But if they disappoint you, it really hurts. And it's worse in a competitive situation because you need to rely on them. You start asking yourself, what let them do that to you? Greg's never told anybody to piss off. He has that view of the world where everybody should do everything correctly; he has that American way, which is charming. But you couldn't go through cycling in that era, with all those demands on you, by pleasing everybody. It just wasn't possible. You were just expected to be an asshole.

"I never realized what sort of pressure and stress those guys who were winning the Tour were under until I noticed in 1990. Riders like that get a basic paranoia. They start worrying about their bikes, their shoes, their tires, their drinks . . . They start saying, I'm going to eat at a different time and have one person doing my bottles. I think Greg was the first person I heard about having one guy do all his stuff for him, like a minder. That's not normal; that's quite shocking. In cycling, though, you realize what you're doing isn't normal: hurting yourself and getting up and doing it again and again."

1984 Tour de France
Millar finished the '84 Tour in fourth place overall, with Greg taking third and winning the white jersey for best young rider. Here, they are followed up a climb by Pedro Delgado. The Spaniard would become an arch rival to both riders throughout the 1980s.

Team: La Vie Claire-Radar

1st: Lisieux (post-Tour criterium, France)

1st: Stiphout (post-Tour criterium, Netherlands)

1st: Tour de France
1st: stage 13
2nd: stages 9, 18, and 20
3rd: mountain time trial and stages 12 and 17
8th: prologue and stage 9

2nd: Coors Classic
1st: stage 5

2nd: Milan–San Remo

2nd: Peer (post-Tour criterium, Belgium)

3rd: Critérium International
4th: hill climb
5th: road race
6th: time trial

3rd: Paris–Nice
4th: stages 2 and 7b
5th: stages 5 and 7a

3rd: Tour of Switzerland
1st: points and combined classification
2nd: prologue and stages 3 and 6
3rd: stage 1
5th: stage 2

4th: Championship of Zurich

4th: Giro d'Italia
1st: stage 5
2nd: stage 16
4th: stage 9
5th: stages 12 and 14
7th: stages 11 and 19

4th: La Flèche Wallonne

6th: Vuelta a Valencia
1st: stage 4

7th: Étoile de Bessèges

7th: UCI Road World Championships (Colorado Springs, Colorado)

11th: Tour of Flanders

14th: Liège–Bastogne–Liège

19th: Gent–Wevelgem

30th: Paris–Roubaix

38th: Rund um den Henninger-Turm

Tour of Ireland/Nissan Classic (abandoned)

Tour de France
In 1986, La Vie Claire was far from being a happy ship. The two Bernards (Tapie, left, and Hinault, right) introduced Greg to the scheming side of bike racing.

Colorado
Greg on his way to—or from—Europe once again.

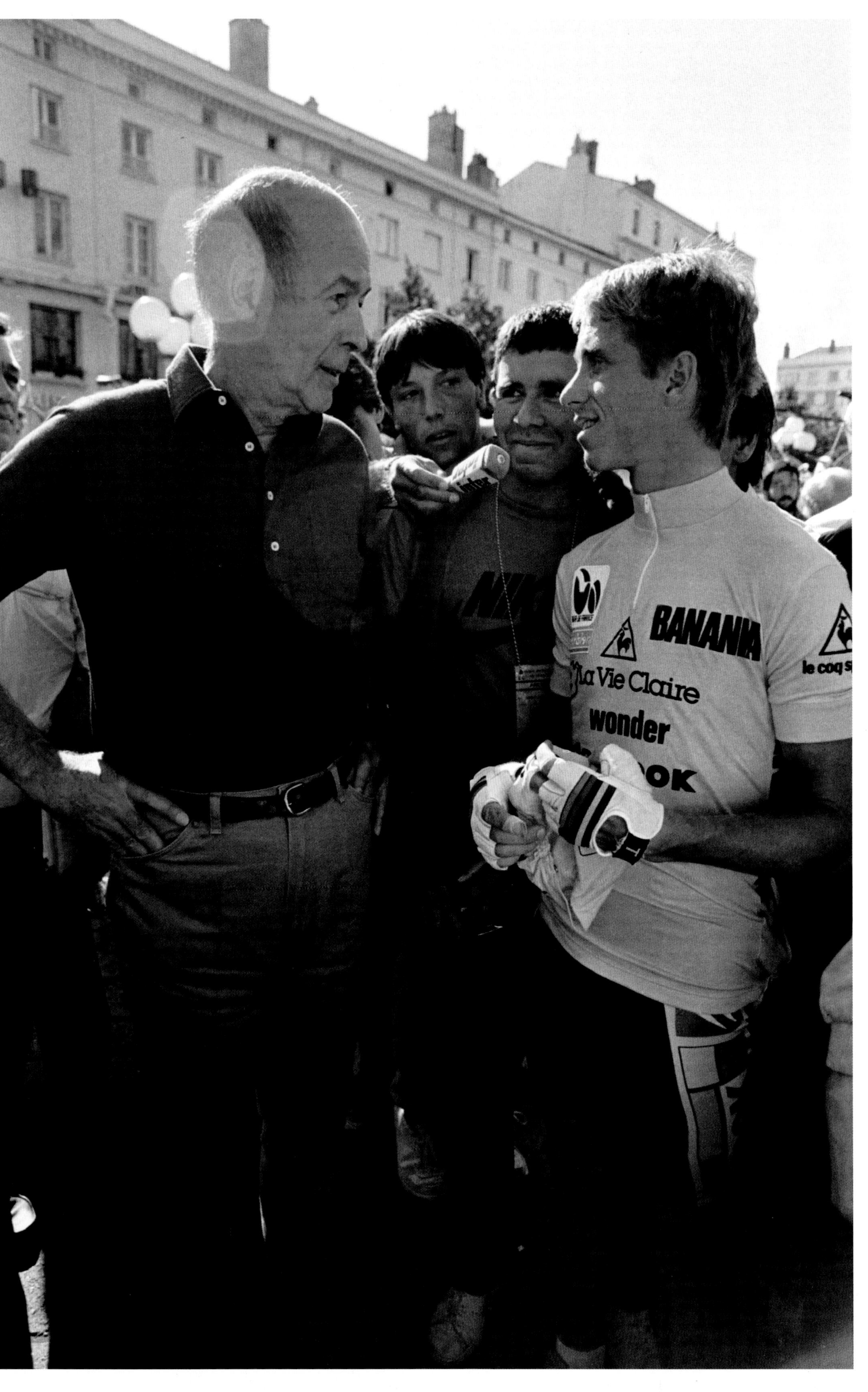
BANANIA
La Vie Claire
wonder

Tour de France
Despite meeting such figures as Valéry Giscard d'Estaing, former president of the French Republic, 1986 was a year of ups and downs for Greg. His growing popularity in France was down to his respect for the language and culture, especially the former: in the 1980s, French was still very much the language of racing.

Étoile de Bessèges
February in the south of France, signing on for the race with former teammates Laurent Fignon and Marc Madiot. The "Star of Bessèges" is a hilly five-day stage race that tests early season form.

Milan–San Remo

The Poggio represents the final chance for the favorites to escape. As the last remnants of an earlier breakaway were being caught, Mario Becca counter-attacked. No doubt the already exhausted Italian couldn't believe his luck when Greg too came over the top of the climb to help on the descent. Sean Kelly, realizing the danger, made an enormous effort to bridge the gap. Kelly would go on to win the sprint on Via Roma.

radar

Paris-Roubaix
Greg's chances of success are ended by a puncture.

Tour of Flanders
"In the '80s, training was all about volume, volume, volume. But volume lowers your testosterone, and it can actually make you go slower. You can, without knowing it, get chronically overtrained and hurt your performance. So, if you're not recovered, you need to take another rest day. In proper training, you don't really train until you are fully recovered."
Greg LeMond

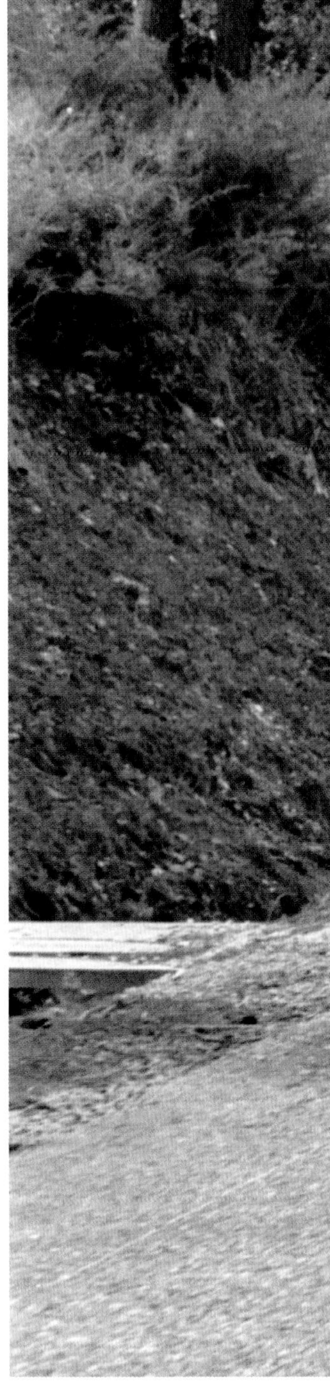

ABOVE, TOP Milan-San Remo
Stretching out the field at Milan-San Remo. This early season stage race in Italy is known for hard racing and harder weather. March in southern Europe can be bitterly cold.

ABOVE Giro d'Italia: stage 5
A rare Italian win for Greg, on stage 5 of the '86 Giro (Nicotera to Cosenza). Employing what French racers call the *Coup de Chacal*, or 'Jackal's Trick,' a surprise last-minute attack in the final kilometers allowing Greg to take a solo victory from the sprinters.

Paris–Nice
"I raced in an era when all the coaches just wanted you to race every race. I should have just skipped a few and stuck with a training ride and recovered completely for the next big one."
Greg LeMond

LEMOND G.
LOCATEL
TOSHIBA
La Vie Claire
WONDER
WONDER
Santini
WONDER
LOOK
Santini

Tour de France: stage 9
"Hinault was the best I've seen him. Despite what had happened before, I was trying to mend our relationship. But had I known what was to come, he wouldn't have been with me on Alpe d'Huez. He was not having a great beginning of the year in '86, but all of a sudden he went to the Tour of Colombia and came back and started racing pretty well. I read an interview with him in *Vélo* or *L'Équipe* where he said, 'Well, we're going to determine the leadership after the first time trial.' But we'd already agreed that I was going into the Tour as leader—that's what we were promised. And then as we got closer and there were more interviews . . . I had no idea what was going on."
Greg LeMond

ABOVE, TOP **Tour de France: stage 18**
"Hinault was saying to me, 'Greg, slow down. My knee is hurting a little bit. Let me ride at my pace. You rest.' So, that's what we did. We went over the hill, and in the valley [Bernard] Tapie says, 'This is Hinault's final win. Let him lead and you come across the finishing line hand in hand.' So that's what we did, because I'm still this 'kid' who wants to make things right with his 'brother.' I wasn't happy. I just wanted to have clarity on how we were racing because, if I'd known what he was up to, I would have put minutes on him on the Alpe d'Huez stage."
Greg LeMond

ABOVE **Tour de France: rest day press conference, Alpe d'Huez**
"Le Tour n'est pas fini . . ." Bernard Hinault and Greg pose for the cameras.

"Hinault had been saying, 'I'm racing for Greg.' But Jean-François Bernard [Greg's teammate at La Vie Claire] said all along that they were trying to screw me. Hinault reinvented it as if he was trying to help me. Tapie just said, 'Okay, let Hinault win.' It was to boost his image. In the valley before the climb, Tapie said, 'Let Hinault win. You get the race, then it's over,' and I said, 'But it's not over until the next race.'"

Greg LeMond

MERLIN
PLAGE
MERLIN
7
Coca-Cola

Tour de France: stage 20
Wearing the yellow jersey with time in hand over Hinault, Greg awaits the start of the final time trial in Saint-Étienne.

"I was confused, angry, and isolated. Yet few people realized how determined I was . . . Anyways, it obviously confused a lot of people. At the time, Hinault said that he was helping me win the race. There were some occasions when it did help, but I would much rather not have had that help; I would rather have raced knowing that we were racing against each other. You'd get the team together the day before the race and [say], 'You get half the team and I get the other, and we're going to race each other.'"

Greg LeMond

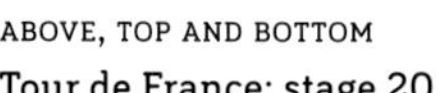

ABOVE, TOP AND BOTTOM

Tour de France: stage 20

There was almost a dramatic finale . . . Paul Koechli and Bernard Tapie look on as Greg and Hinault go head to head at the final time trial. Hinault was the eventual winner, while Greg had to change bikes following a crash. After the time trial, and wearing the yellow jersey, Greg said to the press: "It's a bittersweet victory, and it's hard to be happy right now. I guess I'll be happy once we get to the Champs-Élysées, but there's so much pressure. There's been so much tension in the air."

Tour de France: stage 21
A puncture and a change of bike on the final stage. This time, the team—including Hinault—would wait for Greg. It was to be the American's first Tour de France.

ABOVE, TOP AND BOTTOM

Tour de France

Victory celebrations in Paris before a very frosty looking dinner.

Tour de France: stage 21
At the finishing line in Paris. To Greg's right, in glasses, is Fred Mengoni, the Italian-born New Yorker who cofounded the USPRO cycling organization in 1985. America's first Tour de France victory was just about to kick-start the US cycling scene.

Lisieux: post-Tour criterium
"I'd had 130 days of racing before September 1st that year, and all of them were raced to win. None of them were criteriums. I did the Giro, the Tour of Switzerland, the Tour de France, the Coors Classic, and in all of them I was trying to win. I just got burned out and I paid the price at the Worlds."
Greg LeMond

ABOVE, TOP

Tour de France: Paris

It's all over and Greg's looking far more relaxed. Here, he's wearing the combined jersey, given to the leader of all the race classifications: points, mountains, and overall.

ABOVE

Lisieux: post-Tour criterium

As per the script, the racing would be fast and frenetic—but Greg would win.

TOP Tour de France: stage 18
A truce is declared over a shared drink. The Badger, however, couldn't be written off just yet . . .

ABOVE Hôtel de Ville, Paris
Greg and Bernard stand united. But for how long?

Greg at San Francisco International Airport.

"If someone told me I couldn't play golf during the racing season, then I'd go play it right in their face. I never played golf at the Tour, but so what if I did anyway? It didn't replace my training; I was still doing twenty to twenty-five hours a week. And probably, golf was the best thing I could do . . . I'd play right after the classics, on one of my rest days. I found it actually to be, at least for me, the best form of recovery because usually on a rest day I'm depressed with fatigue and too tired to really go riding. So I'd just go out and walk eighteen holes and I'd get out and breathe and . . . recover. That is still absolutely relevant today. Nothing has changed. Physiology is physiology.

"In '86, on a rest day at the Coors Classic, Hinault and I were just sick of each other. So I went out and played nine holes and I sat in the car. He was all in to win in his last race. But our team went out, and at the time it was fractured and the atmosphere was awful. I couldn't wait to pack up for the year. I'd just won the Tour! The Coors was like my vacation, right? On my rest day, I just went out and played golf—nine holes, an hour and a half. I'd got into golf a couple of years before, and I was passionate about it. I came back to the hotel, and Hinault had just got back from a three hour ride. I didn't believe in doing a three hour ride on rest days. I believed in doing an hour at a good tempo, and I'd already done my one hour ride.

"Hinault and Jean-François Bernard met me in the lobby. They were so mad that I was not doing everything I could to help, you know, 'to win the Tour'—going out with the team, making sure. So I said, 'You just wait till tomorrow. I'll be fine; don't worry about it.' The next day, I was asked to spark up a very hard circuit race with a steep hill, and I played a little game that Hinault had played with me in the Tour, where he attacked but claimed he was helping me soften the opposition—which he wasn't. So I followed every break in there, and I followed Phil Anderson . . . Hinault could not keep up with me. At first I tried to establish just a two minute lead. And then the coaches were telling me, 'You can't ride, you can't ride!' So I told Phil, 'You just keep up and I'll help you win the stage, don't worry.'

"Hinault got off his bike and threw it down, saying, 'You've got to help me!'—just like a little kid. And so finally I said to Phil, 'I can't ride, I can't. I got to slow down. I got to go back.' So we got absorbed. But then, as we got absorbed, I just kept following every attack. Jean-François Bernard kept coming up and pushing me, saying, 'Bastard! You're not helping Hinault!' 'No,' I said. 'You were no good to me on the Tour in '85, and that's exactly what Hinault did to me on that Tour. You're getting some of the same medicine back!' After all, I gave him that race."

Greg LeMond

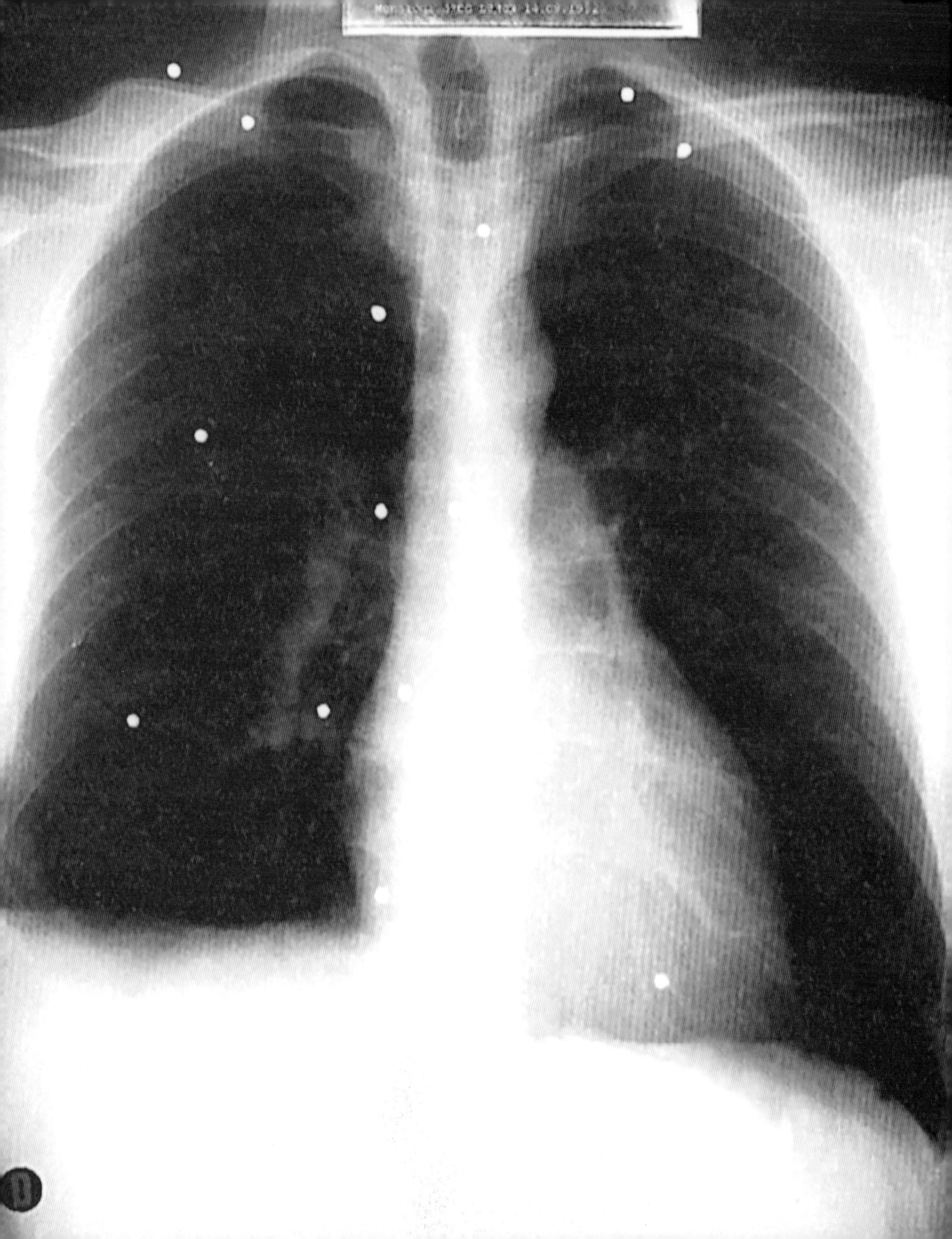

"In professional cycling, no one is ever asked, 'How do you feel?' or 'How are you doing?' even. And that's not how I am. I really love people, but I couldn't always show it."

SHELLEY VERSES

April 20, 1987

The day after Moreno Argentin won the hilly Belgian classic Liège–Bastogne–Liège, Greg went turkey hunting with his uncle and brother-in-law, Pat Blades. Greg was back in the United States recovering from a broken left wrist he'd picked up in a crash at Tirreno–Adriatico earlier that season. During the hunt, the three men became separated. Pat heard something move behind him, so he turned and fired. Greg was hit from behind and at close range, the buckshot penetrating his back and right side.

Greg's injuries were severe. He lost about seven pints of blood, his right lung collapsed, and his diaphragm, intestines, kidney, and liver were all damaged. Worse still, two pellets had lodged themselves in his heart. If he didn't receive medical attention soon, he would almost certainly bleed to death. The men were miles from anywhere on a ranch in the foothills of the Sierra Nevada in Lincoln, California, about a hundred miles east of San Francisco. Luckily, using a cell phone, they managed to contact emergency services, and a police helicopter arrived to take Greg to the medical center at the University of California, Davis. There, a team of three surgeons, led by Dr. Sandy Beal, operated on Greg for more than two hours. They were unable to remove all sixty of the pellets in his body, however, as many had landed in vital organs, and the risk of further injury was too great. Which is where Greg picks up the story . . .

"I've got thirty-five lead pellets in me. They're still there. Three in my heart, five in my liver. One pellet is right on the main artery, in the middle—a hundredth of a millimeter and I would be dead. And the surgeon said, to get those three out, just those three, I'd have to have had open-heart surgery.

"After the accident, there was never any doubt: I just wanted to get back to racing. It was a far more serious accident than I ever let on, because no team would have given me a ride . . . And barely a month into recovery, La Vie Claire contacted me, saying, 'Thanks a lot and goodbye,' so I had no job. Bernard Tapie sent me a letter saying I was fired and they stopped paying me. I wasn't sure if I would race again. Physically, I went from about 150 to 121 pounds in a matter of two months. That meant I had atrophied 30 pounds of muscle, and within two months I started riding again. I told my dad to check things out and two teams were interested—Carrera and PDM—and both made an offer. I went with the Dutch PDM squad.

"PDM's contract said I had to race before the end of the '87 season otherwise they weren't gonna sign me. My dad was almost in denial: he was negotiating for me to race in July! The day that he called me, I was in San Francisco and I'd just done my first ride for two hours. We went to Chinatown for dinner, I had this agonizing pain [and it transpired that] I had an intestinal block. I asked Kathy to put me out of my misery, it was that painful. I went into the hospital at five in the morning and the doctor had a new technique. [I thought to myself,] if anyone finds out this is an intestinal block, I'll never get another team. So I asked him to take my appendix out too and I told the team I'd had appendicitis.

"I'd only just done my first race over two hours [on July 11], and it just wiped me out. I pretended I had a flat, but I was dropped from the start. I remember dropping back through the cars and all these directors laughing at me. I did the Tour of Mexico that year, too: 8,000 feet of climbing. I kept riding as much as I could; I even did the six days of Grenoble. It was insane. I was getting used to getting dropped. [There were] no years until 1991 where I felt 100 percent healthy.

"When you lose 70 percent of your blood volume, it takes months and months to build back up again.

PREVIOUS SPREAD
An X-ray showing some of the gunshot pellets lodged in Greg's body after the shooting accident.

What I realized was that the first blood test I ever did was in '89, two years after the accident. It was in the middle of the Tour of Italy, to check my iron stores, and I needed iron. I had never had an iron injection, so that was my first injection of any vitamins. When your body rebuilds that much loss of blood, you basically utilize iron. I needed to take iron the whole time to help rebuild the red blood cells, the hemoglobin. I took a multivitamin pill and that's it . . . I had zero iron stores. You can have hemoglobin in your red blood cells and still have red blood cell volume, but if you have no iron in your hemoglobin you cannot carry oxygen. So that's part of the struggle I had for two years. I had no iron; I had no oxygen carrying capacity caused by the loss of blood.

"I'm 100 percent certain that the pellets left in my body had [a negative] effect, especially toward the end of my career—absolutely."

"I just could not keep up. I'd started doing VO2 max testing, in '89 before the season. After '91 and '92, I did it in January too. Then, in '92, I quit the Tour and we noticed a drop of about 10 to 15 percent in my oxygen consumption. I couldn't even start the Tour in '93, and the moment I started back in the peloton I could feel myself getting worse and worse. I did another test, and this time I had about a 20 percent drop in oxygen. By '94, I'd spent three years changing every type of training I did: one year I trained no cyclocross, less cycling, then more road riding. Over a couple of winters I trained harder than I ever trained, and in the February races I'd just get blown away. Nothing was logical: I couldn't figure out why, in the '80s, I'd do less training and be competitive.

"In '94, I made it to the Tour de France, but it was as though I had a limiter on me for oxygen: I just couldn't get enough. So I quit after six days, and this time I went home for more tests. At that time I thought it was lead poisoning, and I had every blood test you could think of: parasites, disease, hepatitis . . . But everything was great; I had 'high normal levels.' The doctors said, 'We don't know any history of lead affecting humans because it gets encased in scar tissue, so that shouldn't be a problem.' In '93, I went to see my old ADR team doctor. He was the only guy in Belgium that I knew to go and ask for advice. And I went in and asked him, did he know who I could talk to about looking into my fatigue. He said, 'Greg, you don't have any pain. You know what, you need to go and see Dr. Ferrari [laughs]. The best is Dr. Ferrari—then you don't have any problems.' He also said that there was a doctor of chronic fatigue at the University of Brussels, Kenny de Meirleir.

"Eventually, I got the diagnosis of mitochondrial myopathy. It's a rare disease that's believed to have a lot to do with many different chronic fatigue disorders. They said it's a degenerative disease, and most likely will get worse. So, when I announced my retirement, I got letters from people with the condition who were in wheelchairs, saying it'll get worse at forty-five or fifty. That made me a little depressed.

"A few years back, I got a letter from some guy who was in a robbery—he was a victim, somebody shot him—and he described symptoms that I'd had for ten or fifteen years. And he was told again that he had no health problems, that the body encapsulates [the lead pellets] within scar tissue, and he started doing blood tests. And every year his lead went up. That only confirmed to me that I had been 'leaking' lead, probably from the time I started racing again after my hunting accident, and that that was affecting my whole immune system. That's why I had this yo-yo effect: I'd have good periods and fatigue periods. Nowadays, if I ride my bike, I keep it short and intense. So, I do an hour of intervals and I feel great. That's why I don't believe it's a degenerative disease, because by now I should be using perhaps a crutch or even a wheelchair.

"My dad was a shooting champion at fourteen years old, so my family was all about target shooting. I've been shooting since the accident, although I haven't hunted for many years now. But in company I make sure we are far enough away from each other. Hunting is more about just being together with your friends. But I like trap shooting, I like target shooting . . . The only thing I really like to hunt is pheasant, because I like eating them. And when I got shot, they [parts of the media] said I pretty much deserved it because I played golf and I ate cheeseburgers and pizzas and drank beer!

"Stress and trauma have a huge impact on the human body, and your body doesn't forget. After you have so many traumas and the stress of coming back so soon [after being shot] . . . Well, I can't believe I did it. I'm lucky I'm alive."

The Show Must Go On

Shelley Verses is a soigneur, one of those essential cycling team all-rounders who's expected to serve as a physiotherapist, massage therapist, coach, chef, driver, medic, psychotherapist, and confidant. Often, the "swanny" is the glue that holds the team together and the shoulder for the wounded or exhausted rider to lean on. In 1985, Shelley was the first woman soigneur working on a European-based professional cycling team. In fact, Shelley was the first woman to work on a European-based professional cycling team, period.

The very same year, Shelley made history. Jim Ochowicz and his 7-Eleven cycling team arrived in Europe from the United States to become the first American sponsored team to compete in the Grand Tours and the classics. 7-Eleven had some very capable riders on its roster, many of whom had raced with Greg as amateurs and followed him into the professional ranks. The team had some early wins, and they certainly looked the part, all of which helped them make a mark. But by their own admission, they struggled to compete at the highest level, being underfunded and outgunned by the more experienced European teams.

Shelley and 7-Eleven traveled to Europe in the wake of a handful of American riders and a select few English-speaking riders who had trail blazed the professional racing scene in the early 1980s. These talented riders managed to make the grade, but, in the xenophobic and cruel European cycling peloton of the time, still had their own problems to deal with. But whatever difficulties they had to face, Shelley had them tenfold. Not only was she American, she was also a woman. And in professional cycling, that meant a whole lot more.

Shelley was recruited by the Toshiba-La Vie Claire team, run by Bernard Tapie and Paul Koechli. They wanted to boost the public image of the team, to match its results, and to do this they needed to change the old-fashioned, narrow-minded team personnel; in Shelley's words, they wanted her "to make the riders happier." The "superteam" they constructed for 1987 was based around the reigning Tour champion, Greg LeMond, and it was Shelley's popular personality, boundless enthusiasm, and fresh ideas that made her an essential recruit for Koechli. Unbeknown to Shelley, the Swiss cycling guru also wanted her to weed out the old regime.

1985 UCI Road World Championships, Giavera del Montello, Italy
Shelley and Greg before the '85 World Championships.

1987:
Shelley Verses

"One thing about Greg LeMond is that he's like this most amazing, lovable, child-like character. He's just happy all the time and he's such an easygoing guy. In my day, all the soigneurs wanted him on their massage table, and all the mechanics wanted to work on his bikes. They wanted 'the cowboy' on their team. There's always a funny story behind every rider, and Greg had his share, but what I remember most is that we'd always have to go back to his room and check to see what he'd left behind. After we'd collected the riders' bags and brought them down to the truck, we'd all look at one another and say, who's going to go back to LeMond's room? They'd be two pairs of shoes, a helmet, jerseys . . . It was a treasure hunt, a bit like picking up after a kid.

"I first met Greg through Jeff Bradley, 'Brad-Dog,' who was on the 7-Eleven team I worked for, because he was always training with Greg. So Greg was often on our team's winter training camps, usually at Rancho Murieta in the Sacramento Valley, California. Greg and Kathy had a house there, and so he'd train with us. To my team, he was very much an American brother: we all got on well.

"We'd always have to go back to Greg's room to see what he'd left behind."

"In late 1986, I was signed onto the Toshiba-La Vie Claire team for the 1987 season by Paul Koechli. At the time he asked me, I was so wrapped up with my job at 7-Eleven, I didn't appreciate the intensity of what was going on at La Vie Claire—we were on our own journey—but they offered me a deal I couldn't turn down. It was seven times my salary at 7-Eleven, and with win bonuses too. I wanted to ask Greg what he thought, because I couldn't work out why the

French team wanted me. I remember this one conversation we had, and Greg said to me, 'Paul wants you to come over to the team to change things.' 'Change things?' I asked. 'I can't even speak French!'

"I was so excited because I was going to be working with Greg, the Tour de France champion, and I'd be working on the biggest team in the world."

"Koechli wanted me to make things how Greg made things: American. He wanted to raise the morale of the team and make the riders happier, so I just did what I normally do. I was so excited because I was going to be working with Greg, the Tour de France champion, and I'd be working on the biggest team in the world. But nobody told me what had been going on under the Bernard Hinault regime, and when I finally got to working with the team it was a bit of a shock. I just hadn't realized. I mean, for example, Andy Hampsten had already left La Vie Claire to go back to 7-Eleven, mostly because of the heat between Hinault and Greg.

"Koechli wanted me to be immersed in French, so he wanted me to work with the French riders at first, and not the Americans. He sent me to the Tour Méditerranéen with all the French-speaking riders. And he really threw me down with the dogs too, with a fully French team support crew that included Joël Marteil, Hinault's soigneur from when he was a junior. I'd been instructed to change the food of the riders; they'd had the same feed everyday until then, but it would only change if Hinault said so. In those days, the teams would eat in the hotel restaurant, and only Hinault would decide if they could eat anything different. Back then, it was very different. We would wash the boys' kit in the bathtub, for example. There were no huge buses or camping cars with washing machines; the job was a lot more tactile. We even rubbed their legs outside in the parking lot. There was no hiding away behind curtains.

"There was still a darkness among the team management at La Vie Claire too, although I hadn't realized it until I had to deal with Marteil. He wanted everything to stay the same, and I wanted to start by changing the food. So at the Tour Méditerranéen, he grabbed all the musettes [food bags] I'd prepared for the feed, and all the food for the race day that we'd put in the riders' fresh team casquettes [caps] before the start—they'd collect these and put all the food in their pockets—and he threw them all across the road and then, in front of me and the mechanics, he got in the team truck and ran them all over.

"I felt so helpless. Mike Neel from 7-Eleven had always told me to never show any emotion, especially cry, in front of the riders. On no account must you cause a fuss. So, I cleaned up the mess with the mechanics and went back into the truck and I just made the old food: ham and cheese. After the Tour Méditerranéen, all the riders traveled

ABOVE, LEFT **Tour de France**
The indefatigable, ever-smiling Shelley Verses—the woman who changed the male-centric world of professional cycling forever and for the better.

ABOVE RIGHT
1986 Tour de France
Shelley hands out much-need provisions to the peloton—with Greg at the front.

to a training camp. I'd told Koechli about the food incident. Marteil had a meltdown on me and was sacked there and then and sent home from the camp. Koechli said to me again, 'I want you to make the team happier,' so I said, 'I'll just do what I normally do.'

"It was a great team, though, with some real characters. Riders like Vincent Barteau, who was built like an American football linebacker. Greg could sit behind Barteau and he'd just get powered through the peloton like a plow. Barteau was so comical too, and so focused on Greg. We all realized that Greg was in amazing health and condition at the start of the '87 season, and that meant there was loads of attention on the team as well. Going to the races, we had days when there were thirty-one invitées [VIP guests] on the team for the day, so in the morning I would have to make thirty-one extra sandwiches for the team cars. And then all the riders' musettes needed filling. There were twenty-two staff on the team back then, compared to ninety-odd now on a big pro Tour team. But we still had the same amount of riders. We were working like dogs.

"I have no idea how Greg came back after what he went through in 1987. When somebody is as low as he was, to come back after he was shot and win the Tour de France? Twice?! . . . That's the sign of a true champion."

"So we were all set to go into the '87 season with Greg as the team leader, and the main objective was the Tour. The team morale was great. Then Greg crashed and broke his wrist at Tirreno-Adriatico. But that's okay; riders crash and they break things. They heal twice as fast as you and me, so he'll be back in four weeks. And then he got shot.

"With Greg came this extra sense of ease. It really made the dynamic of a team—that cowboy feeling again—but suddenly not having Greg there really changed things. The team carried on, but it seemed weird. It was like a family member had just vanished. But he's lying there on a hospital bed and it was clearly very bad. He lost so much blood; he nearly died. His lungs collapsed and his body is full of shrapnel. And all the team management will say is, 'Don't worry, Greg's going to be fine.' In those days, even if a rider died, we weren't allowed to talk about it. Just don't upset the riders, was the message. It's the strangest thing; people don't talk about it. 'Keep the horses quiet and carry on.' It flips from one plan to another overnight: we have this budget for these races, and we just have to keep going.

"Even weirder was, nobody contacted him. The team didn't pass a card around the bus to sign, and nobody called Kathy. Nobody on the management told us how he was, even. Because we're a pro team, and our team owner has decided we carry on. It was like flicking a switch. Greg was like, gone.

"After that, Greg couldn't make the Tour and so Bernard Tapie flicked the switch on Jean-François Bernard and made him the new team leader for the Tour. So we all had to take up our parts. It was chaos for the team at the Tour, and how J.-F. managed the pressure I'll never know; I mean, he didn't even ask to be in that situation. Of course I wanted J.-F. to win, but the feeling was that the Tour missed Greg that year. When Greg got hurt, it hurt the Tour too, and there was no sense of fair play at the Tour in '87: no Hinault, no Greg, no *patron*. It just wasn't the same.

"I'm sure that Greg came back too early that year. He was there for the Tour of Holland, and one night after a stage, he was on the massage table and I noticed something really odd. I was massaging his left wrist, working on the bones he broke earlier that year, when I noticed there was some irritation on the skin of his forearm, like an allergic reaction or ingrowing hair or something. I asked him if he'd changed arm warmers or jersey fabric or anything different, and he said that he hadn't, but that it's really hurting. I took a closer look. Under the surface were tiny shards of metal coming out of his skin. Presumably they had been in there, under the plaster cast, since he had been shot. Soon after, Greg went home to rejuvenate his body properly. He came back later in the year, for the Nissan Classic in Ireland, but for La Vie Claire . . . well. Tapie was away thinking he'd found the next Bernard Hinault in J.-F. Bernard.

"It's not when the great champions experience victory, it's when they experience defeat that really shows who they are. When they have to dig so deep into their reserves, when they have to pick themselves up and push themselves so hard to come back . . . The way Greg dug into himself is beyond what any words can say. It's different from the pain of a hard day on the Gavia, or six hours training in the rain, or starting a classic in filthy weather with 200 riders and only 27 finish. I honestly don't know how Greg did it. Seriously, I have no idea how he came back after what he went through in 1987. When somebody is as low as he was, to come back after he was shot and win the Tour de France? Twice?! That's about as deep as you can go. That's the sign of a true champion."

"Greg was so good tactically; he was playing all the time. He was so relaxed—watching breakaways, watching alliances. Even with Italians, where he didn't understand the language, he'd know when a breakaway was going to work. He'd smell it."

ANDY HAMPSTEN

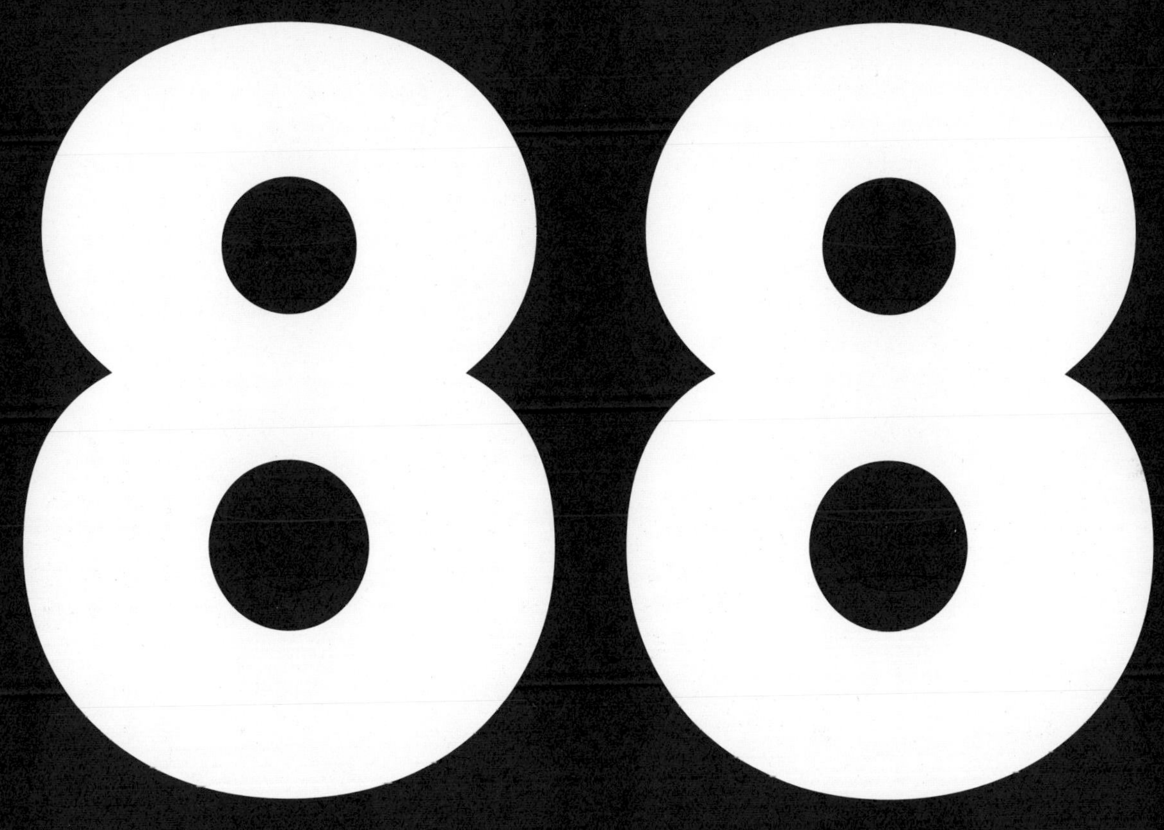

PREVIOUS SPREAD
1986 Tour de France
The La Vie Claire American contingent at the 1986 Tour, with Andy Hampsten on domestique duty for Greg.

ABOVE **1981 Tour de l'Avenir**
The American team was strong and competitive, even with Greg now riding for Renault. Alex Stieda (far left, with his back to the camera) and Andy Hampsten led the line.

The Only Way Is Up

Andy Hampsten first came to notice in the 1985 Giro d'Italia, when he won stage 20 riding for the 7-Eleven team as a stagière (a rookie professional with no full-season contract). Overall, he would finish that year's Giro in twentieth place, an impressive result indeed. Greg, Bernard Hinault, and the management of La Vie Claire also recognized how good Hampsten was. Greg, in particular, wanted him on his side for the 1986 Tour de France.

In what would be Hampsten's first full year as a professional, he turned out to be far more than just a useful rookie and teammate, finishing fourth in Paris after a bruising Tour de France. It was an astonishing performance: first-timers rarely finish a Tour, let alone compete for the podium. Added to this was a win at the Tour of Switzerland earlier that year. The collective eyebrows of the team bosses had been well and truly raised: Hampsten was going to be good. In fact, in the eight times he competed in the Tour de France, he finished outside the top twenty only once (and then only just, coming in twenty-second in 1989). What's more, he was on the starting line for eight consecutive Tours, from 1986 to 1993, finishing fourth twice.

Winning the Tour of Switzerland twice and the Tour de Romandie once proved Andy's excellence in races that involved plenty of climbing. A Tour de France stage victory at the top of Alpe d'Huez in 1992 was one of his Tour highlights—the victory that many pure climbers, like Andy, cherish. He was a consistent rather than attacking climber, and knew how to time his efforts perfectly. Always relaxed, his expression hidden behind a pair of Oakley Factory Pilots, his calm exterior hid an ambitious and competitive rider, one who never seemed to panic. This tenacious fighting spirit, combined with a highly tactical dress sense, led Andy to prevail in the 1988 Giro d'Italia. He attacked the frozen and exhausted race leader Franco Chioccioli on the Gavia Pass in blizzard conditions, dislodging the *maglia rosa*. He then defended his newfound lead all the way to the finish, despite a late rainstorm during the final day's time trial in Vittorio Veneto (where his main rival, Urs Zimmermann, crashed spectacularly in the slick conditions).

Andy's Giro d'Italia victory was a popular one in Italy, especially as no Italian rider had seemed likely to challenge his lead. He was duly adopted as one of their own, and remains the only American ever to have won the Giro.

At the start of his racing career, Andy had to leave his native America in search of bigger goals. Like Greg, Andy wasn't really suited to the racing in the United States in the mid-1980s. Apart from a couple of stage events, most were flat criteriums or road races on short circuits. Andy was built for the mountains, and had the perfect physique for the European races, especially the Grand Tours. So traveling to where the races went up into the mountains was how he began to shape his career.

1988: Andy Hampsten

"As an amateur with the USA team, I could travel to spring races in Italy and France and winter races in Central and South America. The Tour de l'Avenir in France was the best for me to do—there were some professionals there. I didn't know I was good enough to be professional, but I was thirtieth in 1982, at the Tour de l'Avenir that Greg won. I liked the rhythm of the race, and I knew that's where I wanted to be. It wasn't until I turned pro for the '85 Giro, and was able to land a one month contract with 7-Eleven, that I met up with Greg again. I remember he told me, 'Hey, Andy, great to have you here! I miss English-speaking guys, so glad you could finally make it! This style of racing will be good for you!' And then he'd tell Bernard Hinault and his team, 'Watch the kid: he's really good!'

"So then in 1986 I signed for La Vie Claire. Hinault was saying, 'We're all here to help Greg win the Tour

1986 Coors Classic
Greg and Andy give the Badger something to chase.

de France.' And then the press began asking Hinault stuff like, 'What are the nicknames of the new guys?' Hinault says—probably on the spur of the moment—'[Andy] bounds up the hill like a rabbit. Let's call him the little rabbit, *le petit lapin*.' [Hampsten's real nickname was actually Ernie.]

"I never understood the economics of 'selling' a race. From my point of view, surely you would have been paid so much more over the years if you'd won races?"

"That year, we'd had a nice winter training camp in Serre Chevalier. We were supposed to be skiing but there was no snow, so we'd do silly things instead. We had no bicycle training during that camp—it was fun. They purposely put Hinault in a room full of bunk beds with myself and two other Americans, Roy Knickman and Thurlow Rogers, who had this guest status at La Vie Claire. They were part of the Levi's-Raleigh team in America. I was La Vie Claire full time when I raced in Europe, but for the Coors race I could race for my old team [Levi's]. But they purposely put Hinault in with us because we were the most rookie. He answered any questions we had, and he couldn't have been nicer. At the races, Niki Rüttimann, who was his favorite helper, he'd always bail him out on the mountains. He was leading, and Hinault couldn't have worked harder to crush everyone, so Claude Criquielion couldn't attack and take the win. It was fun then—really good camaraderie, really fun at the table—and it taught me a lot.

"I had a three year contract with La Vie Claire, but I left because I didn't want to be the 'Greg' having to deal with Jean-François Bernard at the 1987 Tour de France. I couldn't stand the tension from that one race. It spoiled things for the rest of the year. I can't believe I left. Paul Koechli was still good. It certainly showed me . . . It was my first full year as a pro in 1986, and if that's the way things were run, I didn't have the stomach for it. So it was hard leaving La Vie Claire. I can't help but wonder how it would have gone, but I couldn't stand that tension again.

"I never understood the economics of 'selling' a race. From my point of view, surely you would have been paid so much more over the years if you'd won races? I only understood it from Greg's point of view: the more you win, the more valuable [you are]. So how can you afford to sell a race? No one was paying a year's salary to throw a big race. The policy at 7-Eleven Motorola was: you can never sell a race, so buy one, if you can!

"So the riders could talk among themselves and make deals on the road, where we could negotiate. There was no deep checkbook for us to buy races with, though, and also the language barrier [was an issue]. I remember Mike Neel at the '88 Giro. I was leading the King of the Mountains, and Emanuele Bombini from Gewiss-Bianchi had been leading before, so Mike said, 'As a backup, why don't we ask Bombini if he could win the King of the Mountains?' And I said, I didn't really trust them to help us. If we go hard, no one from Bianchi is even around, so I don't see the point. It came down to some later stage: Bombini was shelled, and I ended up winning the King of the Mountains anyway. I'm a bit of a 'one in the hand is worth two in the bush' kinda guy. I loved the king of the mountains prizes. I've always been very skeptical doing business deals with teams . . . In '85, we were asked who our captain was, and Bob Roll [Hampsten's teammate at 7-Eleven] responded, 'We're all captains!' We were all trying to win, which Italians didn't do. That really changed in the '80s, and certainly into the '90s. There were a lot of domestiques trying to win a stage at the Tour de France and Giro to double their salary on another team.

"At the '86 Tour, I wasn't torn over who to work for, but I was naive—and Greg certainly wasn't—on Hinault's tactics. Up to the mountains [stage 12], we had a great race. We did a horrible team time trial, though; I'd love to know what actually happened there. We worked together so poorly: it was amazingly bad. We did quite a bit of attacking early on in the race, to keep people nervous, but Laurent Fignon's team [Système U] tried to out-Hinault Hinault and set up echelons where there wasn't enough crosswind. They tried to strong-arm us and intimidate us, and we were just able to sit in second position and laugh at it and not get into any difficulty. At the first time trial, both Greg and Hinault did so well. I can't fault Hinault for winning it—he has to go as fast as he can, it's a time trial—but that first day in the mountains, that's when my confusion started. But I guess my point is, at the finish of that day, I sort of swallowed Hinault's line of 'we always race aggressively, that's just what we do.'

"To put more detail on it, during the first climb, there must have been twelve or fifteen riders in the front group, but Hinault was holding that group and we still had two mountains to go. And he was just sort of sitting at the front with nobody off the front. And I thought, if Hinault's pulling, then I should be pulling, because Greg and I were there [from] La Vie Claire. So I asked Greg, 'What's he doing, because obviously I should go do it [too],' and Greg said, 'I have no idea what he's doing!' So I pulled up next to Hinault and said, 'What are you doing? I'll pull if you want me to pull.' And [he replied with] some obscenity; I wish I knew what he said to me. I pulled a little bit, not necessarily off my attack, but he did his attack soon afterward. But it was a very good attack. Our opponents had to chase it down, or wait for their domestiques to come and chase it down and really tire themselves out. Greg was smart enough to take off and recoup some of the time toward the end.

"Greg reacts to situations. He was very conservative with his huge resources, which for a teammate could sometimes be very frustrating."

"I stayed with Greg, and then our rivals were chasing things down. I think it was ours to pull, thinking, this is great: when the break's caught, then we'll attack. But I'm a timid climber. I didn't want to do it so much the first day, which is why Hinault attacked. If I'd have been thinking just about the team, I'd have thought, this is great: our B-plan is working out. I felt terrible for Greg. That night at dinner, Greg was distraught. I recall there was tension, but it was, 'Great, we're racing.' The atmosphere was, 'That was plan B. Look how destroyed everyone was chasing us! Look at the results sheet: first day in the mountains, blowing the race apart like we always do.' But Greg knew Hinault was going after it, and I just swallowed the line.

"Greg reacts to situations. He was very conservative with his huge resources, which for a teammate could sometimes be very frustrating. Maybe because he studied the sport so much, he really wants the attack to be perfect. And he's intellectually so active in his mind that he's going over all the scenarios . . . A good example was the 1986 Tour de France. I've already been dropped before we go up Luz Ardiden, and Robert Millar is bringing me back on a false flat. So I'm drafting, I'm eating, I'm coming up on the LeMond group, but it's a long straight and I can see them. And I can 'read' Greg. He's bouncing, twitching, he feels so good, but there's still ten, fifteen kilometers of hard climbing to go. He wants those five minutes back on Hinault. But he's with Urs Zimmermann, Erik Breukink, Pedro Delgado . . . very good riders. And right as we rejoin—and they don't see us coming—we make a right hand turn. So straight away I attack up the steeper route. It looks dramatic, because they pause quite a bit. It looks like I'm taking off for the victory, but I look Greg in the eye and say, 'I know you need me to attack. Come on, I'll help you.' And that's exactly what happened. He so appreciated me attacking Zimmermann, Breukink, and co, and then he could counterattack and take off for the victory. He knows he's going to win.

"Greg was nervous, though, and he wasn't enjoying it. That day, Bernard Tapie flew in by helicopter, and he's saying, 'Sort out this situation.' The Swiss guys are distraught. I'm sure the French guys are distraught too, and I'm asking Koechli, 'Hey, this is terrible. What's going on? What's this second attack?' And Koechli is honest. He says, 'It's for Greg, but [Hinault] is doing his own thing. I can't reach him.' After the stage, we're getting our massages and going for dinner, and it's only our team at this little hotel. So the riders are there—waiting for our food, of course—and when Hinault comes in, he sits at one end where there are French guys near him. They all whisper, 'What did Tapie say to you?' [And Hinault indicates,] 'It doesn't matter.' And Greg comes in, and Steve Bauer, and I ask him the same. He says, 'Oh, Tapie loves it. He says he'll straighten [Hinault] out.' But we all know he won't do anything.

"The tension was horrible. There were two Swiss guys sitting in the middle of the table . . . It should be hilarious, but there's no food, it's just this horrible suspense in the air: you could hear a pin drop. But after three minutes of that, Greg is tearing up the baguettes and making dough balls, throwing them at teammates, and starting to play around. And then Tapie walks into the room, larger than life, and the riders start to talk a little bit about the results, the stories, etc. As a minor side note, I took over the white jersey from Jean-François Bernard, who did a good race, but I finished top ten. So I'm doing alright, I moved up . . . Anyway, in *L'Equipe*, there was an interview with Tapie where he says, 'When Bernard brings the white jersey home to Paris, he's the great hope of French cycling. I'm going to give him my Porsche 911.' Right on! So Tapie's walked in, doing his thing, but we all know he has nothing to add to this crisis we're dealing with. And out of the deadly silence, Greg asks him straight: 'Hey, Tapie. Now that Andy has the white jersey, are you gonna give him your Porsche?' And two Americans and one Canadian are laughing their asses off, and that's about the only noise in the whole room.

"I'd no idea if Greg was coming back after he was shot, or if he could make it even. He was so miserable. He did the Giro in 1988 . . . and it just hurt to see him. He didn't finish, but myself and everyone on my team were just hoping he'd come back to racing well again. It was such a shock. We were always delighted to have him around, but it was funny for me racing with him when he was injured, trying to keep his spirits up and keep him in one piece, because it was so hard for him to be that weak.

I think he did the Giro again the following year too, as preparation for his Tour comeback win.

"My theory about Greg: I think he's the strongest rider I've ever raced with. Stronger than Hinault, [although] I think Hinault was more tenacious. Greg is the physically most gifted rider I've ever seen. Since he was such a good junior, had so much talent at the beginning, I think he had a difficult period in the years he was injured by not training enough. He'd do huge rides in Belgium: seven or eight hours with Steve Bauer and Phil Anderson and thirty-three degrees. He had no problem doing the workload . . . He'd probably only go golfing three times a year, but he was in all the newspapers for months and infamous for doing things other than riding his bike. He was so strong at everything that in his mid- to late twenties, he was going to have some missteps anyway. I have a theory that, especially if someone sprints well, those talents fade and you need to replace it with more horrible work. And I think he would have been slow to recognize that. Then he's injured and putting on weight. He would go to the Giro and lose all that weight, calories, but in Italy there's no pressure. So we're having fun, and the food's great. We Americans love racing in Italy, because you can be in a crap hotel but the food's gonna be great. And you go downstairs and there's really nice people to chat to and have a glass of wine with. For someone like Greg, who's under so much pressure on the Tour, going to Italy is like a breath of fresh air.

"I saw him really limping in Italy [during] those years, though, trying to beat his weight. In '89, at the Tour DuPont in the spring, right before the Giro, he'd already been injured and trying to come back for two years. But he loved that duel; he loved the challenge of coming back. He had those nice handlebars. We'd have conversations with him: let's not use them until the Tour de France, he'd say. It had been really hard seeing how much he was suffering, but then great to see it all come together on the Tour.

"For me, winning the Giro was very much 'the foreigner winning in the land of the Mafia,' but my take on it is that it was easier for me to win that Giro than any Italian. They would always say in *Gazzetta dello Sport*: 'Now that there's a foreigner in the lead, we'll form alliances and bring the victory back to the motherland . . .' It's the greatest lie! There's no way Italians are going to work together! Gianni Bugno and Claudio Chiappucci will never work together. They were really good friends, but they played in a silly game where they had to have battles. I'd line up with them and they'd have these conversations: 'Did you say that about me?' But I paid attention. I had good politics, I had friends on Italian teams who would tell me my gears were wrong—they helped me keep that race. But I never had any indication that an 'Italian Mafia' was going to do anything. I wasn't very worried. Racing in Italy was fun. I didn't like racing in Belgium, though; some races would stress me out more than others.

"Greg picks up on everything French. His French was always very good. It took me years to get that good, quite a while to understand what was happening. Once Hinault was out of the picture, there might have been a French mafia waiting to do something, but they didn't really have anyone to work with. And it was pretty chaotic between all the countries. Racing in Italy was chaotic—but with incredibly good races—because there wasn't the same pressure from sponsors in the north. Usually, if there was one or two French teams at the Giro, you'd have to be careful, because half of the team would be so bummed out. They had to live outside of France for three whole weeks . . . When I went back to the Spanish team Banesto, it seemed like this "superteam," but they were so horrible outside of Spain, strangely and genuinely uncomfortable—even in Italy!

"Greg was so good tactically; he was playing all the time. He was so relaxed—watching breakaways, watching alliances. Even with Italians, where he didn't understand the language, he'd know when a breakaway was going to work. He'd smell it. He was strong enough [that] he could play around at the back and get to the front in time to see what's going on. He was very good at reading races because he could relax so much. He genuinely enjoyed doing it."

Team: Toshiba-La Vie Claire

19th: Omloop Het Volk

44th: Nissan Classic/Tour of Ireland

Team: PDM

2nd: Deurne-Zeilberg

2nd: Sospiroli

2nd: Tour of the Americas
2nd: stage 4
3rd: stage 7
4th: stage 6b
5th: stages 1 and 2

3rd: Grand Prix de la Libération TTT

5th: Grenoble Six-Day (with Tony Doyle)

12th: Baracchi Trophy (with Peter Stevenhaagen)

30th: Tour of Flanders

44th: Tirreno-Adriatico

46th: Nissan Classic/Tour of Ireland

94th: Paris-Brussels

107th: Volta a Catalunya

Four Days of Dunkirk, Giro d'Italia, UCI Road World Championships (Ronse, Belgium), Vuelta al País Vasco (all abandoned)

1987 Toshiba-La Vie Claire team presentation
The riders pose with Bernard Tapie—and a bike.

UCI Road World Championships, Ronse, Belgium
Greg consoles his friend and longtime teammate Steve Bauer after his disqualification in the controversial sprint-finish crash with Belgian rider Claude Criquielion.

Tour of the Americas
A seemingly relaxed Greg LeMond with Davis Phinney and members of the press.

Tour of Flanders
"When you don't have the conditioning, or if you've been away from cycling for a long time, you forget how much cycling hurts. You really forget."
Greg LeMond

Milan–San Remo
Still competitive toward the end of the longest single-day spring classic on the calendar, the 294 kilometer Milan– San Remo, also known as "La Classicisima di primavera." Hot on Greg's heels is Laurent Fignon.

Milan–San Remo
Greg stayed with the move going up the Cipressa climb, but with around thirty kilometers to go, he crashed out of the race on the descent. Fignon was the eventual winner.

Tour of the Americas
One of Greg's best performances of 1988 came on home soil.

Nissan Classic/Tour of Ireland
It's September, it's cold, and Greg is running out of season to find his form. He eventually finished in forty-sixth place, noting at the time: "I did better than half the field. A lot of people finished behind me." His liaison with PDM would be brief.

Giro
BOTTECCHIA

“We had a good team at that time . . . the atmosphere was really great, and we had somebody who was able to gain us a lot of publicity. For the opening few days, we were as strong as anyone. And for a team time trial, we were perfect.”

JOHAN LAMMERTS

PREVIOUS SPREAD

Paris–Roubaix

Like many of the races in the 1989 spring campaign, the "Hell of the North" would be a hell of a struggle for Greg.

ABOVE

Training in Mexico in 1991.

Good-for-Nothings

Picture the scene: you're a roommate of a Tour de France team leader, arriving at the hotel after yet another stage, tired, sweaty, and hungry. Your roommate finished so far ahead that he's already on the massage table and you're still in your bib shorts, sitting on the bed, staring into space. Exhausted, you struggle out of your kit and into the shower. Two people living in the same room, but existing at different ends of the race and worlds apart. But another day is done, and you're another step closer to Paris . . . Throughout the last century of racing, most team riders have approached the Tour de France as if in a war of attrition. Forget winning: all but the best riders are just in survival mode.

A cycling team is a peculiar beast. The elements that make it work well are complex and hard to define. Behind the talent of the leader has to be a perfect mix of support riders, each with considerable talents themselves, but all happy to put aside their own ambitions for a single rider, the strongest rider—a rider like Greg LeMond. Professional riders learn their strengths and weaknesses the hard way, in what can only be described as a brutal and unforgiving apprenticeship. To make it into a team, you have to prove yourself as an amateur, perhaps by being a national champion and performing well at the World Championships. To make it into the Tour de France, you have to race at the highest level as a professional against the best riders and hold your own. So let's be clear about this: there are no bad riders at the Tour de France, not even average ones. These guys are at the top of their game.

The late 1980s were something of a watershed for Belgian cycling. Gone were the dominating riders of the '70s and their winning ways—riders like Eddy Merckx, Michel Pollentier, and Lucien van Impe at the Grand Tours, and Roger de Vlaeminck and Freddy Maertens at such one-day classics as Milan–San Remo in Italy, Liège–Bastogne–Liège in Belgium, and Paris–Roubaix in France. Belgian teams, ADR included, struggled to gain sponsorship, and in 1989 they badly needed a winner. To realize that need, they looked mostly for riders with something to prove. And, although he would sign very late, almost as the 1989 season began, Greg was one of them. It had been a tough time for the American, with a difficult couple of years behind him, so he was put on a reduced salary and given the incentive of win bonuses for a variety of races and competitions, including the World Championships, the Tour de France, and reaching number one in the World Cup, the season-long best rider competition. The ADR team manager, José De Cauwer, had negotiated the deal, which stated that Greg would receive a bonus (around 6 million Belgian francs, or €150,000) for each victory. Most thought that De Cauwer's money would be safe; even Greg didn't think he'd be asking for a check for 12 million Belgian francs at the end of the season.

The ADR team had become known by the less than sympathetic Belgian fans as "Al De Restjes," which, loosely translated from the Flemish, means the "Good-for-Nothings." Yet despite being written off not only by the fans but also by most of the media, ADR was actually made up of some wily and useful professionals, with the likes of Eddy Planckaert and Frank Hoste riding alongside such lesser-known talents as a very young Johan Museeuw. These were competitors of some quality, although perhaps with something still to prove or yet to be proven. Also on ADR's roster at that time was Johan Lammerts, winner of the Tour of Flanders in 1984. Johan is Dutch, which, in the context of Belgian cycling, is no small matter: of the one hundred editions of the race the Flemish call the Ronde van Vlaanderen (or 'De Ronde' for short), sixty-eight of them have been won by a Belgian. The Flemish always want a Belgian winner, so for an "outsider" to win was a rare event indeed. The fierce rivalry between Belgian and Dutch cycling meant that even the suggestion that a Dutch rider could win the Ronde would be hard to swallow. Johan became one of only nine of his countrymen to win the event.

As the saying goes, "If you win the Ronde, you'll never have to buy a beer in Belgium again." Unless, that is, you're a Dutch winner of the Ronde. However, for Johan Lammerts, a rider who was born in Bergen op Zoom, just across the border in neighboring Holland, and who grew up only an hour's drive away from the start of the Tour of Flanders, winning the race was all the more special.

An annual race, the Ronde has become part of the very fabric of Belgium. The direction signs and arrows painted on the road are permanent reminders of the one day in April that becomes a national holiday; even the cobbles are maintained specifically for the race. It's an incredible event to watch, but not so enjoyable to ride: there's nowhere to hide, and only the strongest and cleverest prevail. In '84, Lammerts outfoxed a group of particularly strong and intelligent riders to take his victory, throwing in a classic late attack that left the final selection of five riders (four Belgians and one Irishman, none other than Sean Kelly) looking at the empty road in front of them. In some respects, the nature of Johan's victory made his win all the more preposterous (four Belgians, remember, and one of the greatest ever classics riders), but it proved he was no slouch. Johan's 1984 season also featured a win at his home race, the Tour of Holland (Ronde van Nederland), where Greg finished seventh as the first non-Dutch rider to cross the line. Johan had success at the Tour de France too, winning stage 20 of the 1985 edition, from Montpon-Ménestérol to Limoges, again with a solo attack. After retiring from racing in 1993 with plenty of experience in balancing the various elements that make a successful team, Johan had stints as a team manager and sports director. He now works for the Dutch Cycling Federation as their national road coach.

Before the start of the Tour in 1989, the odds for a LeMond win were a little on the long side. So when he made it to Paris and the final stage with an outside chance of winning, even his roommate Johan thought that victory was unlikely. In fact, nobody, save for his closest family and friends, thought Greg could beat Fignon on the final day in '89, but back then racing was far less predictable. And what happened next was to be one of the tightest and most exciting finales to any bike race.

1990 Tour de Trump
From left: Andy Hampsten (7-Eleven jersey, red sleeves), Johan Lammerts (team Z jersey), a young Evgeni Berzin (the Russian winner of the '94 Giro d'Italia, in red), and Greg.

1989:
Johan Lammerts

"I turned pro in '82, and Greg and I raced together from that point on. At the end '86, Greg was looking for some new riders for the Toshiba-La Vie Claire team, so we talked a bit and he asked if I was interested. I joined the team in '87, and we became teammates from that time. Greg was my team leader, and that sometimes helps someone from the 'second row' like me to try to win a race. And that happened on a few occasions. For example, I can remember the Waterford stage of the Tour of Ireland in 1990 and a stage of the Vuelta a los Valles Mineros in Spain in 1989 when I won due to Greg being the team leader. In a sense, we supported each other like that: Greg helped me as much as he could, and vice versa. He's a very good friend. I've enjoyed spending time with him, and although we don't see each other that much these days, we're friends for life.

In 1989, Greg and I became team- and roommates again at ADR. Behind the scenes, there had been some problems regarding our payments for salaries,

1991 Paris–Nice
Lammerts was renowned for being the cool-headed Dutchman. He was a popular wheel to follow in the peloton, and, in his later career, a loyal comrade to Greg.

etc., and also with joining the Tour through a sponsor—because you had to pay a fee at that time and so on. So we started the Tour . . . and it was kind of difficult due to the money problems, but we had a good team at that time. After the first time trial, where Greg won and took the yellow jersey, the atmosphere was really great in the team, and we had somebody who was able to gain us a lot of publicity. For the opening few days, we were as strong as anyone. And for a team time trial, we were perfect. That Tour had the perfect start for Greg too, because he was very good in the classics, so the cobbled stage 4 [from Liège to Wasquehal] was ideal for us [Johan Museeuw, also of ADR, finished the stage in third]. Greg's confidence was growing, especially as most climbers and team leaders are always uncomfortable with those stages. Afterward, we had to defend the jersey on many stages. It was a strong flat team but not so good for climbing . . . It was very difficult for Greg: he was totally alone in the mountains, and that was a big concern at the time.

"Greg was a smart racer, that's for sure. You still see it in his commentary for Eurosport nowadays: he knows how it all goes."

"In the Pyreneean stage 16, from Gap to Briançon, De Cauwer wanted one of us to go in the break, because between the two big climbs—the Vars and the Izoard—he knew Greg could have been vulnerable to attacks and would need some help in the valley. Eddy Planckaert was sent first, but he punctured, so I had to attack hard to get in that group. I made it over the Vars in the front, but I was caught by Greg's group on the descent and I rode as hard as I could to keep it all together. Those things happened, but it was tough because of the lack of climbing ability of most of our team. And we were only five riders for the Pyrenees, and only four of us made it into Paris: René Martens, Johan Museeuw, Greg, and myself.

"However, the difference was only in the mountains. Laurent Fignon had a stronger climbing team, so the 'only' thing Greg had to do was look at Fignon and some other good climbers, and that was it. But Greg knew that, in cycling, especially on the climbs, you are most of the time on your own anyway. If you have a good team around you, of course it can help you a little bit, and you can have help in the valleys where you have to regain time, but in general, you are on your own.

"Greg was a smart racer, that's for sure. You still see it in his commentary on Eurosport nowadays: he knows how it all goes. The Tour de France is about both attrition and tactics. A three week stage race is always tactical. You have to be good in the first week, but you have to be excellent in the last week. The harsh stages are in the final week, where there is a possibility of making a difference in the mountains, but you have to be strategic; you have to think about where you'll make the difference. And Greg was excellent at that: he knew when there was a stage coming up where he could make a difference [between him and his] opponents. Those are the good riders, the ones who can think strategically and tactically and, at the moment when it counts, use their physical abilities. That's how they win races.

"Of course, nowadays in cycling, there's a lot more money. Budgets are bigger, and the riders are focused on just a few races in the year. When we were racers, we had sometimes 140 racing days; now, riders have less than half that [amount]. They train more than race. They have altitude camps, etc.—there's quite some difference. Cycling itself, in a sense, is still the same. There's a start and a finish, and the big classics are absolutely the same. The Tour de France is still the same too, although they have one more rest day and they ride about 600, 700 kilometers less. So in our time, we simply rode stages more easily than they do these days! Things are different now, but that's the way it goes. It has evolved. The point is, the unpredictability has gone a little, and we should get some of it back. These days, because of the shortening of races, the roles and tasks riders are doing are much more defined.

"If you think about that last day in '89, it seems very difficult now, when he was still fifty seconds back from Laurent Fignon . . . It was almost impossible to win that Tour de France, but he did it. Maybe it had a little to do with Fignon not using the aero handlebars, but that was his choice; he had them but he didn't use them. Greg just had an excellent performance in that time trial, one of the fastest time trials ever done in the Tour de France [at 54.5 kph, it remains the fastest time trial over 20 kilometers]. The way he was at that moment was, 'I can win another stage,' not 'I can win the Tour de France,' and that's what he was doing in a sense. He did that, and was a little bit surprised he regained the loss he had suffered the days before. That was a remarkable thing."

Team: ADR-Agrigel-Bottecchia

1st: Amiens (post-Tour criterium, France)

1st: Callac (post-Tour criterium, France)

1st: Emmen (post-Tour criterium, Netherlands)

1st: Lèves (post-Tour criterium, France)

1st: Linne (post-Tour criterium, Netherlands)

1st: Tour de France
1st: stages 5, 19, and 21
4th: prologue and stage 16
5th: stages 15 and 17
6th: stage 18
8th: stage 9
9th: stage 10

1st: UCI Road World Championships (Chambéry, France)

2nd: Brienon-sur-Armançon (post-Tour criterium, France)

2nd: Châteaulin (post-Tour criterium, France)

2nd: Maarheeze (post-Tour criterium, Netherlands)

2nd: Trophée du Centre à Montluçon (post-Tour criterium, France)

3rd: Tiel (post-Tour criterium, Netherlands)

3rd: Tour of the Americas

4th: Critérium International
2nd: road race
8th: hill climb

4th: Grand Prix des Amériques

6th: Tirreno-Adriatico

7th: Vuelta a los Valles Mineros

10th: Tour of Philadelphia

17th: Omloop Het Volk

39th: Giro d'Italia
2nd: stage 22
8th: stage 4

63rd: Tour of Flanders

113rd: Classica San Sebastian

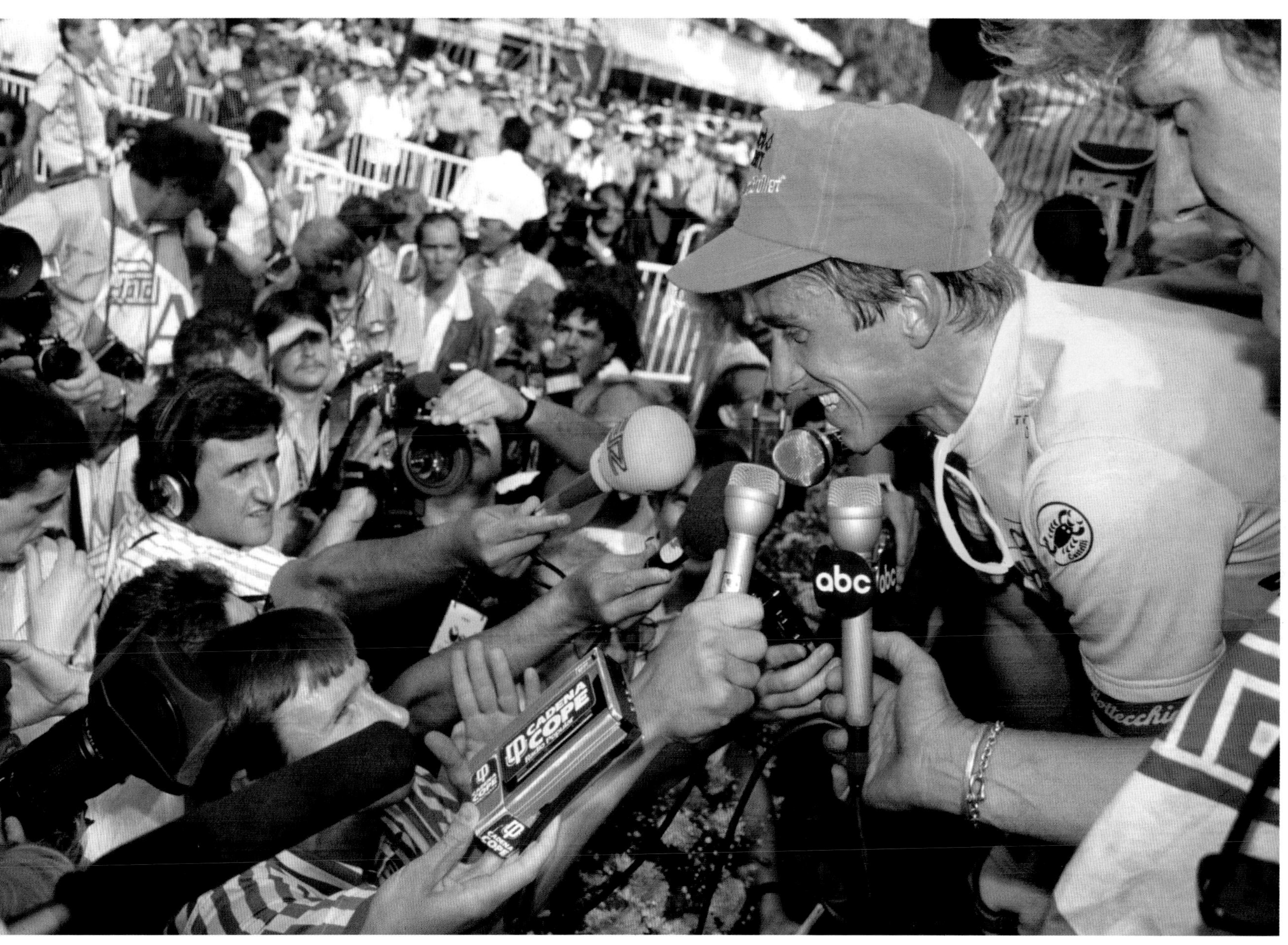

"When I won the Worlds in 1983, our neighbors in Kortrijk planted four flags outside our house: the US flag, the Lion of Flanders, the Belgian flag, and that of the town. In 1986, when I won the Tour, there were people camped out in front of the house for days. And after the Worlds in 1989, they painted my name on the streets."

Greg LeMond

ABOVE, TOP

Omloop Het Volk

Off the pace and out of sorts on the Muur van Geraardsbergen.

ABOVE

Paris-Roubaix

A few weeks later, at Paris-Roubaix, and the form had not improved.

"For me, it was a tough year, because I had honestly wanted to quit cycling in April, because you can only take so much . . . But I raced a lot more than I thought in 1989. Johan Lammerts was my best friend and most loyal teammate during those years. He was a great support. It was a dark year. I got sixth place in Tirreno–Adriatico, but I had allergies, iron deficiencies . . . And I hadn't been paid at all at that point, and the stress was on me. I was gonna quit, I was so frustrated. Then I finished well in the last time trial at the Giro."

Greg LeMond

Tour de France: stage 8
From left: Colombian climber Luis Herrera, Tour de France director Jacques Goddet, Laurent Fignon, Father Joseph Massie (priest at the Notre Dame des Cyclistes in La Bastide d'Armagnac), and Greg.

Tour de France: stage 5
In terms of confidence, the time trial around Dinard was a pivotal moment for Greg. He wasn't just going well, he was smashing his way through the field and about to catch former teammate Christophe Lavainne. Greg won the stage, beating his rival Laurent Fignon (who finished third) by almost a minute, and taking the leader's yellow jersey. Perhaps this was a taste of things to come.

"When you look at the time trial at the end of the Giro that year, Laurent Fignon and I were on the same equipment. And then I took 1 minute 21 seconds out of Fignon, and then I'm thinking, in theory, I'm in better shape . . ."

Greg LeMond

ABOVE, TOP

Tour de France: stage 2

Despite the outside criticism, ADR managed a pretty good team time trial in 1989, losing only fifty-one seconds to Fignon's well-organized Système U squad.

ABOVE

Tour de France: stage 5

On stage 5, the first time trial proper, Greg won by twenty-four seconds, with Pedro Delgado in second. He also put fifty-six seconds into Fignon, who finished third.

Tour de France: stage 17

Everyone, even the best riders, have a bad day at the Tour. In 1989, Greg's was the stage to Alpe d'Huez. Knowing Greg so well, it was Laurent Fignon's team manager, Cyrille Guimard, who noticed that the American was suffering, pulling alongside and telling Fignon to attack with four kilometers to go.

Tour de France: stage 16
With Greg in yellow, it was looking like a stalemate. It was certainly getting tense, with all the favorites looking at one another.

PIC DU MIDI-2877M

Tour de France: stage 10
"The reality is that Fignon lost that Tour himself. On the Tourmalet, at the most critical time when it was really going hard, he was getting dropped. I turned back and he's sitting there holding on [to a motorbike]. So we get to the end of the stage and he beats me by ten seconds, and then he's saying to the press that I'm not racing like a true leader for the yellow jersey! Now, I hadn't been at the front on a mountain stage since '86, and my only memory of it was getting blown off on every frickin' mountain, and I don't even have a teammate to help. The next day, I said, 'Listen, you better shut up. I saw it—you were holding on to the motorcycle. That means you're out of the race. It's not like you're a guy in the gruppetto trying to get over a mountain. You're in the front and trying to win the Tour.'"
Greg LeMond

ABOVE, TOP

"[Fignon] congratulated me on my second place the day before but, to myself, I said, 'You arrogant so and so . . . you're gonna lose it.'"

Greg LeMond

ABOVE

Tour de France: stage 17

All hands to the pump after a puncture. It was Eddy Planckaert who gave up his wheel to keep Greg in contention.

Tour de France: stage 17
Down but not yet out . . .
At Alpe d'Huez, Greg lost the yellow jersey. Everyone, apart from him, thought he'd also lost the Tour.

Tour de France: stage 21
After almost 3,300 kilometers of racing, Greg won the '89 Tour by eight seconds—the equivalent of a mere fifty meters. The deficit overall had been fifty seconds after stage 20, and over the twenty-one kilometers of the final stage, his chances were slight. As Greg pushed on to the finishing line, he almost caught Pedro Delgado, two minutes ahead and, ironically, the pre-race favorite. Afterwards, Greg said, "All I could think was how terrible it would have been to lose by one second." Cyrille Guimard, now Laurent Fignon's manager, made a complaint about Greg's handlebars, but the judges were happy for him to use them. The protest continued post-Tour, but the commissaires pointed out that Fignon had the option to use them too. Nevertheless, time trials at the Tour de France would never be the same again—and there's never been one on the final day since.

"I didn't think. I just rode."

Greg LeMond

UCI Road World Championships, Chambéry, France
As if the hills of the Rhône-Alpes weren't bad enough, the weather was dreadful. Only forty-two riders would complete the race. Martin Earley leads Marino Lejarreta, Steve Bauer, Claude Criquelion, Laurent Fignon (obscured), Sean Kelly, Gianni Bugno, Greg, and Rolf Sørensen.

UCI Road World Championships, Chambéry, France
"I really didn't think I was going to finish the race. I felt terrible that day, but you don't 'just quit' the Worlds. I'd thought about winning, and I imagined myself winning, so I thought it was possible. During the race, I felt so bad. I was ready to quit, and each lap I was just saying to myself, one more time, one more time . . . I had broken my back wheel, and with two laps to go I was going to stop and change it. But I thought I'd better not: a lot can happen in the last two laps. In that moment I started feeling good. And it worked out."

Greg LeMond

ÉDITION
LE TOUR
Les stars
Les engagés
Les équipes

"My job was more to be a free agent, and basically to attack and upset the other teams, so that's what I did . . . Of course, when I made so much time on the first stage, the original plan changed somewhat."

RONAN PENSEC

PREVIOUS SPREAD
Despite Greg's victory over a French rider, the 1989 Tour had been the most exciting for years. And in France, Greg was gaining quite a following.

ABOVE Paris–Nice
Ronan Pensec, with big hair and an even bigger headband, at Paris–Nice. Roger Legeay, team manager at Z, takes notes.

Business as Usual

Throughout the '80s and '90s, Ronan Pensec was a familiar sight at the head of a bike race. The Frenchman was always a feisty competitor, what his compatriots would call a *baroudeur* (literally, a fighter or a warrior). Ronan was noticeable too, with his penchant for a large quiff and sideburns. If there's ever been such a thing as a rock 'n' roll cyclist, then Pensec was probably it—an animated character both on and off the bike. At his first Tour de France, in 1986, he finished sixth. A remarkable achievement for any rookie at the race, it underlined his climbing abilities and strength for stage racing. Perhaps France had found its next Tour winner.

In 1990, Roger Zannier, owner of the Z clothing company and main sponsor of the Z cycling team, had half-joked with his riders about his preference for them not winning their respective national championships. These races were usually held the week before the Tour de France, which in 1990 started on June 30. Zannier's was an international team, with several Frenchmen, a Briton, a Norwegian, and an American in the mix, but he wanted every member of his team to be wearing the distinctive, Pop art–inspired Z jersey of his clothing chain; winning a national championship meant wearing the colors of one's country. "Who cares about the British, the Norwegian, or the French champion at the Tour de France?" he is alleged to have said. "And those at the side of the road don't really care either."

Zannier is even believed to have joked about Greg LeMond's 1989 World Championship rainbow jersey, which he would wear throughout his debut year with team Z, describing it as "upsetting" the team photographs. This emphasis on "team" wasn't just a marketing gimmick, however. Roger Legeay, the legendary directeur sportif, made sure that team Z was built around some strong and consistent riders, rather than outright superstars, and the spirit he nurtured was instrumental in the team winning the 1990 Tour jersey and the first team award.

A solid prologue for Greg that year was followed by a bizarre first stage (against an equally bizarre backdrop of the Futuroscope theme park), in which a relative unknown rider went on the offensive in a howling gale. Claudio Chiappucci and his breakaway companions, Steve Bauer and Frans Massen, gained almost eleven minutes on LeMond and the rest of the overall favorites. The one lieutenant that Greg knew would police the move and look after his interests ahead of his own was none other than "Rockin'" Ronan Pensec. In cycling, this audacious attack would usually be known as an *échappée bidon*, an early or "soft" breakaway, set up for lowly riders or to give teams some TV exposure. Sometimes, such breakaways are used for tactical purposes, to take the pressure off the team leaders or sprinters. In this case, it made no sense whatsoever, and proved to be a lasting move for Chiappucci—one that took team Z the entire Tour to topple.

In many ways, the stage 1 result played into team Z's hands perfectly, with Pensec's high placing overall allowing them to leave it to the other contenders' teams to chase and follow the moves. In a three week stage race, being on the defensive early can be both mentally and physically exhausting for the team and its leader. By the end of stage 12, little Claudio replaced Pensec as race leader, and was well on top of the GC and looking good—although stage 13 was certainly going to be unlucky for this yellow jersey. In a tough stage through the searing heat and vicious hills of the Massif Central, the diminutive and inexperienced Italian missed the move. A break formed, and his team fell apart trying to catch it. Isolated on the road to Saint-Étienne, Chiappucci's lead withered a little, and the organized might of team Z began to take control.

1990:
Ronan Pensec

"Greg could have had many more victories. For him, the Tour de France and the World Championships were always most important, but he could have won many classics—the Giro perhaps, the Vuelta a España too if he'd wanted—because Greg was a very special athlete, a cut above the average rider. I remember the first time I saw Greg race. It was at the Ruban Granitier Breton, which was a big amateur race in my hometown of Douarnenez, so I went to watch. It was the summer, and I was still a junior racer. I remember Greg was wearing the USA team jersey, and was not yet professional, although I think he had already signed a contract with [Cyrille] Guimard to ride for Renault, so it must have been 1980. [In fact, this race was just before Guimard signed Greg for the Renault team late in the 1980 season. The American Olympic team had pulled out of the Moscow Olympics, and so Greg had decided to turn professional. Guimard had been following Greg after his win in the Junior World Championships the year before, and, despite the American's less than professional decision to quit

Tour de France team presentation
The team Z riders line up for the crowds at Futuroscope.

the Ruban after a puncture and a slow wheel change—Greg is still angry with himself for throwing his bike at the team car—the Renault team boss was keen to recruit him. In fact, Guimard was reported to have said, "Now I want him. He's got character, but no more nonsense like that."]

"I remember the first time I saw Greg race. It was at the Ruban Granitier Breton, which was a big amateur race in my hometown of Douarnenez, so I went to watch."

"My first Tour de France was in 1986 with Peugeot. Although I was very much on the outside, you could see that things were tense at La Vie Claire. But we had no idea what was happening inside the team; you only knew about your concerns. It was their problem, so I wasn't too worried about Greg in those days. I was surprised when Hinault attacked on the stage to Superbagnères [stage 13]. I remember I was angry too, but only because I didn't have the opportunity to get into the break that day myself!

"Greg joined Z in 1990. The team was always like a good group of friends. We'd all ridden together for a very long time, and we were professionals doing our jobs. So with or without Greg, the morale was always very good. It's in my nature to smile and have fun, and there were never any conflicts between the riders that I remember. By 1990, I was one of the longest standing riders at the team, and so Greg was the new boy. We first raced together in the same jersey at the Tour Méditerranéen in 1990, where I was in the yellow jersey early in the race.

"Greg is a very nice guy, and his friendly personality made it easy for him to fit into the Z team quickly and become a part of the group. Everyone knew their place in the team, and that's very important, because tensions appear in a team when somebody doesn't know their role or thinks they can be the leader, but doesn't have the capacity to do it. But in the case of Z, that didn't happen: we all knew what we had to do. To support Greg, Roger Legeay decided that it was best to have mostly strong climbers in the team for the 1990 Tour, with only a handful of rouleurs added for the flat stages. We had Gilbert Duclos-Lassalle, François Lemarchand, and Bruno Cornillet, who were all strong riders, to do that job on the flat. When these first riders were tired, there was Jérôme Simon and Atle Kvålsvoll to take over. And then there was Robert Millar, who was a very experienced climber and had been a team leader also, so he understood what Greg needed. Alongside Millar there was Eric Boyer and myself for the mountains.

"My job was more to be a free agent, and basically to attack and upset the other teams, so that's what I did . . . Of course, when I made so much time on the first stage, the original plan changed somewhat. But when I wore the yellow jersey, there were never any tensions between Greg and I. Naturally, the team helped me win the jersey and keep hold of it for as long a time as possible, which meant Greg could keep out of trouble, and that worked really well. Because for the first two weeks of the Tour, Greg had very little pressure. By the stage 12 time trial, Greg had clawed back a lot of time but was still a long way behind Chiappucci. I lost the jersey that day.

"Then, after the rest day, there was stage 13 from Villard-de-Lans to Saint-Étienne. I was a little bit sick with bronchitis, but I went on the attack early and made it into the break. It was only a small group but, for me, this was perhaps the most important moment for Greg's win at the Tour that year. Chiappucci's Italian Carrera team had to ride all day in the front, behind the break, to protect the jersey. Just before the final climb, the Croix de Chaubouret before the finish in Saint-Étienne, the break was caught, which meant that Greg could then counterattack Chiappucci, who by this point had no teammates left and was really tired. This attack enabled Greg and some other contenders to gain back much of the time they'd lost on that first stage.

"We had a small panic on stage 17, when Greg punctured on the Col de Marie-Blanque and we all had to wait and chase back on, but we were always in control. By the time we got to Paris, we'd only lost one rider, and 1990 was what all sponsors dream about. It was a really good race for team Z, because we won the team award, I had the yellow jersey [for a while], and of course Greg won it in the end. I've remained in touch with Roger Zannier, and he still says that the win in 1990 was a very emotional moment for him. He talks about it as one of his finest personal achievements."

Tour de France: stage 1
The breakaway. From left: Frans Maassen, Steve Bauer, Claudio Chiappucci, and Ronan Pensec. Maassen won the stage, while Bauer took the leader's yellow jersey.

Tour de France
From the "Good-for-Nothings" in '89 to the "Good-for-Everythings" in '90 . . . Team Z on the podium in Paris. The team had been put together specifically to win "La Grande Boucle."

Team: Z-Peugeot

1st: Dijon (post-Tour criterium, France)

1st: Lombron (post-Tour criterium, France)

1st: Tour de France
2nd: prologue. and stages 11 and 16
5th: stages 7, 13, 14, and 20
10th: stage 10

2nd: Alcobendas (post-Tour criterium, Spain)

2nd: Barentin (post-Tour criterium, France)

2nd: Championship of Zurich

2nd: Château-Chinon (post-Tour criterium, France)

3rd: Châteaulin (post-Tour criterium, France)

4th: UCI Road World Championships (Utsunomiya, Japan)

6th: Bol d'Or des Monédières (post-Tour criterium, France)

10th: Tour of Switzerland

91st: Clasica San Sebastian

105th: Giro d'Italia

Critérium International, Paris-Nice, Ruta del Sol, Vuelta a Valencia (all abandoned)

Tour de France: stage 2
Despite consisting of some very talented riders, team Z was found lacking on the day and lost a minute to Panasonic, finishing seventh.

"I'd lost confidence from '86 on, because my experience at the Tour de France [that year] was about absolute suffering. In 1990, though, I won with a ten minute deficit and I didn't suffer at all. I was flying in the team time trial practice, and I knew I was 'on.' Three or four days into it, the pace was so high—I'd never seen it so consistently high."

Greg LeMond

ABOVE, TOP AND BOTTOM

Tour Méditerranéen: stage 3

Ronan Pensec had won stage 2 the previous day, and was wearing the leader's jersey. He would eventually finish fourth overall.

Tour Méditerranéen
"I was in bed for the whole of April. I started feeling better after being off my bike for five weeks. Then I got top ten in the Tour of Switzerland. Ideally, you're always at your best form, but if you've got talent, you can still do it at 98 percent."
Greg LeMond

Tour Méditerranéen: stage 5
The time trial through the streets of Hyères. Sick and out of sorts, Greg decided to pack up, go home, and recover.

Paris–Nice: prologue
The start of the "Race to the Sun." This, however, was to be another abandoned event for Greg, who would fail to make it to the customary finish on the Promenade des Anglais.

"In my first six years of racing, my pre-race meal was you'd get up, have a croissant or a piece of bread and coffee, and then you'd need lunch. The French didn't want to miss their lunch, so it wouldn't be like an American breakfast. They would have just a little piece of bread, which they would normally have for breakfast, but then because they were going to miss lunch, they'd have a full-on lunch served for breakfast instead: steak, or chicken, pasta, salad. I look back now, twenty years on, and it's actually the perfect pre-race meal. You have protein, fat, and modest amounts of carbohydrates, because you don't want to spike blood sugar . . . modest amounts of carbohydrates and refill the tank right after the race, but about three hours before you need to have some substance. In the '90s, there was a craze for low-fat, where Roger Legeay had everyone on a diet. We were doing a tour of Italy, and we can't eat cheese and we can't have olive oil, you can't have dessert . . . I mean, we were starving ourselves. Half of us made it to halfway through the race and we had to quit."
Greg LeMond

Tour de France: prologue
Second behind Thierry Marie in the first time trial stage was another sign that Greg's form had returned at last.

VETEMENTS ENFANTS
MOTO-PRESSE
DIRECTION
EPREUVE

Tour de France: stage 11
Spectators picnic as the 1990 peloton rolls past. Ronan Pensec wears the yellow jersey, with Greg right behind him.

Tour de France: stage 17

On stage 17, Greg's form was returning, but his luck ran out. A puncture on the descent of the Marie-Blanque left him without team support or a spare wheel for about three minutes. Fully aware of the situation, Claudio Chiappucci's Carrera team drove the breakaway, which included most of the top ten riders, onward. The result was a breakneck chase, with Greg making the most of his teammates. Following Greg on a motorbike was Jean-François Pescheux, the then race director of the Tour de France. "I've never seen a descent that fast," he later recalled. "LeMond never braked once. He took each curve at top speed. I thought he was crazy."

ABOVE, TOP

Tour de France: prologue
When it came to aerodynamic equipment, Greg was still ahead of the game. He had his position nailed. The aero helmet, however, was later shown to have cost more time than it saved.

ABOVE

Tour de France: stage 11
On Alpe d'Huez with Pedro Delgado and Gianni Bugno. Further up the mountain, Greg would ride away with Bugno, the stage's eventual winner.

Tour de France: stage 17
Following Greg's puncture, stage 17 became chaotic. Greg had teammates—including Gilbert Duclos-Lassalle in an another breakaway—ahead of the main leaders, so they all had to wait for Greg so they could help re-establish the chase. His rivals weren't about to stop and wait for him at the side of the road, of course, but in cycling there's an unspoken rule that if a rival rider in contention gets a puncture, you do not attack or press on.

Tour de France: stage 17
Team Z brought Greg back up to the Chiappucci group and saved the race. The Italian's actions didn't go unnoticed.

Tour de France: Stage 20
After Chiappucci's attack on stage 17, Greg said, "Chiappucci did an unsporting thing, and in cycling this is not done. I will not forget this; he will pay the bill later." And at the final time trial at Lac Vassivière (above), Greg took the yellow jersey and the race.

Tour de France
In taking the yellow jersey at the final time trial, Greg demonstrated not only his never-say-die attitude, but also how organized and prepared Roger Legeay and team Z had become. Even when under pressure, they didn't need to panic.

UCI Road World Championships, Utsunomiya, Japan
A strong group of chasers was completely outfoxed by a strong Belgian team and a disjointed chase by Rudy Dhaenens, who stayed clear to win. Gianni Bugno won the sprint for third place.

OAKLEY
DUPONT
DUPONT
Tommaso

Greg was a great, great cyclist, and during his days he was a great champion, a great 'Champ'—'Champ' is what I call him, even now."

OTTO JACOME

PREVIOUS SPREAD
1991 Paris–Nice
At the Race to the Sun, as it's known. Greg's form in '91, however, was slow to show.

ABOVE **1991 Tour de France**
Taking refreshments at the finish in Paris. Greg was disappointed with his performance that year, but accepted that his best wasn't good enough.

LeMonster

Cycling's best professional teams and its greatest stars would be nothing without their support staff. They are the unsung heroes of the sport, many of them having given up much of their own lives for the cause of running a successful cycling team. It's an antisocial existence—you're away from your family and friends for many months at a time—and it's usually the soigneurs (literally, "one who provides care") and mechanics who keep the whole thing rolling along. However, they have to be able to do an awful lot more than rub legs and fix chains. With umpteen bikes or nine busted-up riders to attend to, they are rarely able to relax.

Team leaders require a little more help, and often employ their own personal soigneurs, or "swannys" as they are often referred to by the English-speaking riders. These are the people who quite literally pick up after the riders—part personal assistant, part confidant, and often the riders' coach and trainer. On a race like the Tour de France, where things can get very intense, they can also serve as security guard, press agent, and, on occasion, even hairdresser.

Some swannys have built high-profile careers around looking after star riders. Fausto Coppi's legendary swanny was a blind, cigar-smoking man called Biagio Cavanna who had been trainer to many of Italy's biggest stars before "spotting" Coppi. The list of his previous clients includes such legendary riders as Costante Girardengo, Alfredo Binda, and Learco Guerra. Cavanna's reputation meant that, at first, Coppi was in awe of him. He was regarded as a genius with a cyclist's legs, and could supposedly tell, just by touch, if a rider was tired and over-trained or in form and ready to win big. Eddy Merckx's swanny was a man called Guillaume Michiels, a family friend who Eddy had known since he was five years old; Merckx regarded him as his second brother. Greg's teammate at La Vie Claire, Bernard Hinault, always had Joël Marteil by his side, as Shelley Verses alluded to earlier. But when the Badger retired from racing, Marteil followed soon after.

For the riders, the end of a hard-fought race can bring a mixture of anger, joy, and dejection. They are usually very tired and emotional as well, so that first post-race contact can be a mixed bag for the swannys, who wait for their riders at the finishing line. Riders will talk—they *love* to talk—about what happened, about who did what and why, and a good swanny will get to know everything about their rider's mood, personal lives, and relationships with rivals and teammates. In the days before choreographed press conferences, journalists would get to know the swannys quite well; among other things, they could help them work out if their charges were likely to want to chat on the rest day, or just be left alone. They are a rider's guardian angel, offering protection, advice, and unconditional support, and all riders build close bonds with their swannys. Star riders will usually take their swanny with them, to whichever team they are moving to. Such was the case with Greg: on his return to racing in 1988, he brought with him his longtime swanny and friend, Otto Jacome.

Jacome had always been a keen sports fan, and he was talented too, winning a state cycling championship in Mexico at the age of sixteen. He also played soccer, a little tennis, lifted some weights (he was a 1962 national champion in Mexico), trained with boxers, went scuba diving . . . He could also free-dive, being able to stay under the water for more than three minutes. When he and his family eventually settled in San Jose, California, his kids wanted to start bike racing at the local track, which was only three miles away. It was here that Otto and his family met Greg and Bob LeMond, when Greg was fifteen years old.

1991–92: Otto Jacome

"Greg was racing in the same team that my kids were racing with, and right away I knew he had big potential: he was so above everybody else. He was so good, the guys started calling him 'LeMonster,' because we saw Greg on a whole different level as a rider. We watched races where he would lap the field three times. I remember once, at the Butterfly Criterium, Greg goes off the front and laps the field, twice. Then, during the race, he hears that Bob, his dad, got a flat. So he drops back and helps Bob get back on, and still wins solo. Later on, I also took him to racing in Tijuana and to my hometown in Mexico.

"In 1981, somebody invited me to go and watch the Coors Classic, and Greg was already with the Renault pro team. He raced against the Soviets, who were led by Olympic Champion Sergei Sukhoruchenkov. Greg won the race, which at the time was his first big win. Before that, I used to give him a massage once in a while, when he was in the States, and he liked how I did it. Then, I remember he was in the team [La Vie Claire] in the Tour de France. They gave him

1992 Tour DuPont
Otto Jacome in his trademark hat.

a laxative when he was in the mountains. He already had an upset stomach, so it just made it worse. And these things made him want somebody he could rely on. So a couple of years later, after his accident in 1987, he said that he would like me to go to Europe full-time with him, because he wanted someone he could trust. He said I could bring two Mexican riders with me to the team, and one of them was Miguel Arroyo. That's how I ended up with PDM in Holland first, and then with ADR in Belgium in 1989.

"Working for Greg was one of the best things that ever happened to me in my life. I'd never dreamed of being in Europe at the Tour de France; it was too far out of my way of thinking. I did all the training and rides that Greg did—Mexico, Venezuela, USA, all over Europe—and all the races that he did in those years, I was always there. I was living really close to his house in Belgium, and when we didn't go to the races, we were always training . . . every single day. And keeping in touch, of course. In those years, you see more of your rider than you do of your wife.

"In training, Greg always knew what he needed to do and how he wanted to do it."

"Of course, I always tried to protect Greg. I did training rides with him in the car or on a scooter. It was always fun. I remember in Minnesota training one time, and I'm in the car. Somehow I had to stop for something, and he took off! I always worried about protecting him. Anyway, I set off after him, and I couldn't see him. I drove up and down the road, but I couldn't see him from my car. He was hiding in bushes all along and he was laughing at me . . . I really was afraid! Greg was always playing around like that. He hid all his bikes once, at the Tour de France, and he told the DS that they'd been stolen. I remember he would take big risks sometimes too. Once, we were going to take a plane in the United States. He said he had my ticket, but he waited until the very last minute when they were going to close the gate, and so we had to run and run and they let us pass. We only just made it on, but when we got on the plane, then he showed me: my ticket was in Kathy's name.

"But in training, Greg always knew what he needed to do and how he wanted to do it. By the time I went to Europe, he had already been racing a long time. He knew what to do. In a group, he never got behind a wheel; he was always on the front and he pushed the gears pretty good. He rarely asked me what I thought, but in 1990, during preseason training, he asked me how he looked. I said he looked a little fat . . . Greg did not always agree, but those things, I got my nose into them, because I could always be honest with him. In 1991, Greg came back from skiing a little heavier, and I knew it would be harder for him on the climbs. So we did a big winter training ride in 1991, [right across Mexico, and] I followed them on a scooter! At first, Johan Lammerts and the others were all stronger than Greg. He said he was tired and that they were pushing him, but he started getting stronger and stronger, just like during the Tour de France. Greg was always talking to people at the hotel in the evenings, in the lobby, in his room . . . and the next day all the riders were tired and Greg didn't feel anything. He had a lot of stamina when he was in very good condition.

"Of course, one of the things when we started in ADR was I gave him Mexican food. He was using hot sauce, and people told him not to eat that; they always criticized him. But he loves Mexican food, and he says, 'I know that you do this and do that, but what have you done to criticize me?' He could eat anything and nothing would happen. It was really hard to find Mexican food in Belgium, though, even tortillas. Sometimes, we had to go to France to shop for food. One day, Miguel and I were in the apartment, in the kitchen, and Greg came up ready to train. We said, 'We're going to eat, and we're having some cow's tongue.' He looked in the pot on the stove, and I pulled out this cow's tongue, and his face . . . He was really disgusted. So I chopped up the tongue, added a little salsa, some salt, and put it in a tortilla and made a cow's tongue taco! I asked him, 'So do you want to try it?' He thought about it twice and said, 'Okay.' He took the first bite, and another bite, and said, 'Can you give me another one?' One day, a month or two later, I was at his house and Kathy had cow's tongue in the fridge to eat for dinner!

"One of the good things about Belgium is that they have racing every day, Saturday and Sunday, and people from France, Germany, were coming over to race there. So the racing was always very tough. Mexican guys wanted to start slow if it was an eighty kilometer race, but they didn't know that if they lost contact with the peloton in front, after five minutes they would be pulled out of the race! So the guys that came over had a hard time finishing those races. Belgium is very flat, and they have small towns and small houses, and it's so windy . . . The racing is very tough, very hard. There was a lot of hostility toward us [as foreigners], and it took some getting used to. Then there was the different weather, the food, all the currencies. When I got to PDM, I remember they gave me a wallet full of different currencies; it was impossible to know the value.

When we had team meetings, they were speaking Dutch and I couldn't understand anything. I started learning by imitation. But later on, you learn how to blend in there. Like the rest of the swannys, you're driving your car at 170, 180 kilometers an hour, and you can be eating and talking away while holding the steering wheel.

"After the Tour in 1989, we spent fifteen days partying and dancing in the nightclubs until five a.m. Then Greg says one day, 'Enough! I want to get serious and win the Worlds.'"

"Greg nearly packed it all in during the '89 Giro d'Italia. He was coming in in the third or fourth gruppetto every day, and he looked really pale. I told him he needed an iron injection, but he got mad with me because he'd never used injections and he was upset because I was suggesting it. The following day, a doctor from the Giro came over to see him, and they told him the same thing, that he needed iron. He got a jab—iron with vitamins—and the next day he says, 'Hey, Otto. I feel so much better now.'

"Greg started to get fit during that Giro [he finished second in the final time trial], and told me at the end that he thought he could win the Tour, he felt so good. I said of course he could win it. In the long time trial at the start of the '89 Tour de France [stage 5, which Greg won], I followed him in the car and we were going so fast . . . He caught eight riders and passed them.

"In that final 1989 time trial, though, he was so fired up he said, 'Don't tell me no times! I don't want to hear anything from you.' Pedro Delgado was in third place, and took off two minutes ahead. And Greg almost caught him. Everyone had thought that Laurent Fignon would win, so they already had the big champagne bottles and the band to play the Marseillaise for him at the finish. But when Greg came in, I knew he had won. Afterward, when we started dancing with Kathy, it was the best time of all. In 1990, we were in the Champs-Élysées, and Greg was changing his shoes and socks, and I was cleaning him up, and he looks at me and says, 'This Tour was not so exciting, eh Otto? Not like last year!' After the Tour in 1989, we spent fifteen days partying and dancing in the nightclubs until five a.m. Then Greg says one day, 'Enough! I want to get serious and win the Worlds.' That was Greg: he always knew pretty much what and how he wanted to do things.

"Greg really depended on me, and loyalty was very important to him. An American reporter wanted to do an interview with Greg, and we were traveling in Greg's car. When the reporter made his report and [described me as] 'his Mexican masseur, a dark colored guy,' Bob told Greg and Greg told the reporter's editor. He said, 'If you don't fire this guy . . . He discriminated my masseur!' He was very upset. The LeMonds stick up for and defend the little guys, the underdogs, the immigrants, the Hispanics. They're incredible people; they'd defend us to the end. Greg's friend Fred Mengoni gave him a Mercedes when he won the Worlds in 1989, but Fred would always joke with me and say, 'Hey, Otto. You're a little bit too heavy these days!' Greg would look at him and say, 'Hey, he's not heavy!' He'd always defend me right away. He'd always jump in, no matter who it was or what they'd done for him.

"When Greg finished in 1994, I'd really noticed that he was having problems. He wasn't the same guy. He was going from up to down, getting worse in his riding. I thought, it's normal, he wants to retire. I told him, when you leave, I leave.

"The most valued thing I still have from those years is a stuffed toy lion—you know, the ones they got from Credit Lyonnais [the sponsors of the Tour in 1989] for wearing the yellow jersey. Greg was in and out of the jersey, trading places with Fignon, and I remember I'd asked him, 'Greg, can you give me a lion?' And he said that everybody had wanted one: Roger Zannier the boss, the team sponsors, his kids . . . He'd given them all away! Oh boy, I really wanted one, so I asked Greg, almost as a joke, just before the last time trial, 'If you get one more, will you give it to me?' And he says, 'Yes, for sure!' It's probably the most valuable lion in the history of the Tour de France."

1991: Down Mexico Way
As the ride went on, Greg just got stronger and stronger.

91

Team: Z

1st: Callac (post-Tour criterium, France)

7th: Tour de France
2nd: stages 8 and 16
3rd: prologue, and stages 1 and 21
4th: stage 19
9th: stage 13

12th: Tour DuPont

22nd: Tour of Switzerland

33rd: Paris–Nice

55th: Paris–Roubaix

119th: Gent–Wevelgem

Giro d'Italia
2nd: stage 11
8th: stage 2b

Critérium International, UCI Road World Championships (Stuttgart, Germany) (both abandoned)

92

Team: Z

1st: Tour DuPont
1st: prologue

2nd: Tour d'Armorique

4th: Tour of Switzerland
3rd: stage 8
5th: stage 4

9th: Paris–Roubaix

11th: Critérium du Dauphiné Libéré
5th: stage 4

22nd: Milan–San Remo

39th: Étoile de Bessèges

55th: Omloop Het Volk

58th: Paris–Nice

81st: Tour Méditerranéen

Tour de France (abandoned stage 14)
4th: stage 6
5th: stage 9

Vuelta al País Vasco (abandoned)

Gone fishing . . .
Training in Mexico
in January 1991.

1991 Gent–Wevelgem
"It became a nightmare, because I was so used to me being in front and anything else was a failure. I put so much pressure on myself."
Greg LeMond

ABOVE, TOP
1991 Paris–Roubaix
Eddy Planckaert and Gilbert Duclos-Lassalle lead the peloton, with Greg and Johan Lammerts in tow.

ABOVE 1991 Paris–Nice
The Class of '91. From left: Gianni Bugno (partly unseen), Laurent Fignon, Gilbert Duclos-Lassalle, Tony Rominger (the race winner), Marc Madiot, Francis Moreau, Stephen Roche, and Greg.

"When I started riding poorly in 1991 at the Tour de France, I couldn't believe the speed we were going at—how was this possible? We were like, 'This is so fast!' Attack, attack, attack, by all the Italians and Spanish. That was the year when speeds went up so dramatically. I look back on 1991 now and I know that they were most likely just all juiced up . . . I'm not bitter about it, but, at the time, you were thinking, 'What am I doing wrong?' Even back in 1990, I was so used to riding poorly and suffering and then riding well for short periods. That was the hardest part in the last few years [of my career]. We became aware of [what was going on] in 1993, but no one ever talked about the difference made in performance."

Greg LeMond

Tour de France: stage 11
Greg's last ever day in yellow.

"There were no [rivals] in 1989 and 1990, and anyway, I wasn't even at my best. So maybe I could have won the Tour two or three more times. However, in 1991, I was the closest [fitness-wise] to how I had been in 1986—but I got my ass handed to me."

Greg LeMond

ABOVE, TOP AND BOTTOM

1991 Tour de France: stage 13

Despite still being the center of attention, Greg lost any hope of winning in 1991 on the Col d'Aspin. Miguel Indurain simply rode away with Claudio Chiappucci, the eventual winner of the stage. Greg came in more than seven minutes later.

KILOMETRE
PMU
1
PMU
ANTENNE 2
466

1991 Tour de France: stage 13
Exhausted and battered, with tape hanging down from his handlebars following an earlier crash, Greg reaches the *flamme rouge* (a red flag indicating a kilometer to go) on Val Louron. He'd fought to stay in touch with the leaders, making a desperately fast descent to catch up with the breakaways at the foot of the Col d'Aspin, but it was not to be. The break had split and the leaders had flown.

ABOVE, TOP
1992 Paris–Roubaix
Following the moves. With Gilbert Duclos-Lassalle having made his escape, Greg keeps an eye on classics specialists Edwig Van Hooydonck and Sean Kelly.

ABOVE **1992 Tour DuPont**
Back to winning ways on home soil. Greg would win both the prologue and the race overall.

1992 Paris–Roubaix
"A couple of years earlier, at the 1990 Tour de France, I'd flatted and Gilbert Duclos-Lassalle was in an eight minute breakaway and headed into a stage finish he would have easily won. But he pulled back and waited for me, and if he hadn't I might not have won the Tour that year. I told him I was going to repay the gesture at Paris–Roubaix one day in '92. I really felt great and chased everyone down to help Lassalle. That was my most satisfying Paris–Roubaix, even though I didn't win it."
Greg LeMond

1992 Tour de France: stage 13
Despite Gilbert Duclos-Lassalle's best efforts, Greg was toast. He lost forty-odd minutes on Sestriere.

SOMMET 1 KM
MILK RACE
51
51
ENFANTS

1992 Tour de France: stage 13
The final struggle through Italy on a merciless stage to Sestriere. Greg would lose almost forty-five minutes that day, although twenty riders failed to finish the stage.

1992 Tour de France: stage 14
Greg abandons on the road to Alpe d'Huez. Ten other riders go the same way, including Greg's teammate Gilbert Duclos-Lassalle (sitting in the back of the car).

gan
ROCK SHOX

"Cycling is not something that you can just do 'as a job.' It needs all of you."

CHRIS BOARDMAN

PREVIOUS SPREAD
1993 Paris–Roubaix
With RockShox suspension forks at the "Hell of the North."

ABOVE 1994 Tour de France
Chris Boardman, track racer and time trial specialist from the Wirral in Merseyside, North West England, found stage racing a very different prospect altogether.

The Old Pro and the Neo-Pro

On a hot and humid day in Bordeaux in 1993, just before the Tour de France was due to zip past the city's velodrome, a relatively unknown amateur rider from Great Britain was inside, lapping the track at 52.270 kph on his way to breaking cycling's one hour record. Later that day, somewhat nonchalantly, he was presented to the Tour de France crowds by the yellow jersey holder Miguel Indurain. This "unknown" had triumphed at cycling's blue ribbon event, taking on a record that only the bravest and most talented riders dare challenge—a record that Eddy Merckx once held (the hour, he said, had been one of the longest of his career). This was big news indeed.

In mainland Europe and away from the United Kingdom, where cycling was rarely covered in the national media, Boardman's feat was celebrated with front-page headlines. In such sports newspapers as Italy's *Gazzetta dello Sport* and France's *L'Equipe*, his exploits even bumped the Tour off the front page. In the UK, by contrast, cycling was not regarded as a serious sport in 1993, and for that week in July, Chris Boardman was probably bigger in Belgium than he was in Britain.

In 1992, however, Boardman *had* made the headlines, winning a gold medal in the 4,000 meter pursuit at the Barcelona Olympics, Great Britain's first cycling gold since 1920. Cycling may not have been big news in the UK, but the Olympics certainly were. Boardman was very much a technical athlete, and had worked meticulously with bike designer Mike Burrows, sports scientist Peter Keen, and a team of Lotus engineers to create a very stealth-like bike. More importantly, in an era when aerodynamics basically meant tucking your shirt in, Boardman and his scientifically minded friends had introduced a whole new approach to bike racing. Boardman himself broke the world record in the final in Barcelona, and the term "marginal gains" was born.

Despite winning a few road and stage races in his career, Boardman was, by his own admission, a short-distance time trial specialist. And it wasn't all thanks to the Lotus bike he had helped develop: Boardman was exceptionally fast with or without it. As he himself notes, his time trial position was so low that his back was curved in a way that made even the most flexible wince. Here was a rider with a big engine, a fast position, and a turn of speed: the professional teams looking for a time trial specialist formed an orderly queue. Boardman's debut at the 1994 Tour de France was as good as it gets for a prologue specialist. In the 7.2 kilometer test, he set the fastest time, took the yellow jersey, and even caught his minute man Luc Leblanc—55.152 kph was the fastest anyone had ever ridden at the Tour.

Nowadays, Boardman, like Greg, runs a successful bike company that bears his name. He rides a bike still, and is one of the few ex-professionals who have stepped into the world of politics. Indeed, his views on road safety for cyclists and integrated transport are refreshingly joined up. But when he turned pro, his career was still a long way from cycle-advocacy. In 1994, he signed for Greg's GAN team, headed by former Peugeot boss and leading French directeur sportif Roger Legeay. Like it or not, he was about to take a turn away from the track and toward the mountains of the Tour de France.

1994 Tour de France: stage 3

The team time trial at the '94 Tour was a significant event for both Boardman and Greg: it was the former's first as a pro and the latter's last. The team time trial can be brutal. The rules say that five riders have to finish for the team to post a qualifying time, so there's a need just to stay together for as long as possible. Weaker riders are simply left behind: if the mix isn't right, a team of nine can be smashed to pieces after just three kilometers. It was at a team time trial that Greg had started in international competition, learning the trade from former Eastern bloc coach Eddie B., a man who knew how to get the best from a group. So by 1994, Greg had already ridden thousands of kilometers in a team time trial formation. He knew the form.

Professional teams are expected to know what to do when it comes to bike racing, but it's remarkable how few get it right in a team time trial. It was clear from early on that Boardman was losing the leader's jersey, but he didn't want to go down without a fight. Only a few of his teammates seemed interested or able to help out, and there were riders simply hanging on as Greg and Chris swapped monster turns. Every time the TV cameras focused on the GAN team, the yellow jersey would be at the front, leading an echelon of stragglers. By the time the team reached the climb, they were down to six riders. Greg was gapped on the ascent, paying the price for his earlier efforts, but he managed to bridge the gap back to the team over the top of the climb. It's a good job he did, because, on the descent, they lost Jean-Philippe Dojwa to a puncture. Down to five. While many teams look to accelerate into the last section of a team time trial, GAN was seemingly slowing down. Then Eddy Seigneur overdid a corner, so the team had to wait . . . With his few days in yellow done, Boardman's Tour career had got off to a frustrating start. And although Greg reorganized the team and buried himself to the line, it was, perhaps, the American's last significant contribution to a race as a professional bike rider. At times during the event, Boardman had dropped the entire GAN team. For one thing, he was aerodynamically so much better, having his handlebars seven inches lower than those of his teammates.

1993–94:
Chris Boardman

"I didn't get to know Greg until a little bit into that season [1994], because he'd been in the States and didn't come to the winter training camp. But I was amazed at what a lovely, warm, and friendly man he was—so interested and so fascinated by everything. He was just like a big kid. Everything to do with technology and the latest bikes [fascinated him]. I mean, even though he was the team's bike sponsor, he ended up riding a Lotus bike in the time trials. He just loved new stuff.

"At the start of the season, we'd already ridden [a team time trial] at the Tour Méditerranéen, and it was just like a series of guys, in the same jersey, going roughly in the same direction—which was the closest we came to [being] a team. I thought, at the time, well that was just the Tour of the Med, I'm sure for the Tour de France it'll be awesome . . . But we trained the day before, and it was just like a road race really: when people couldn't go through, they just sat-on or got dropped. Afterward, I thought there would be a debriefing or discussion, about what we did wrong or what we could do differently, but we simply climbed off the bikes, someone said 'Lunch?' and that was it.

"We were embedded in a very traditional team who had no appetite for change, so we had to beat them over the head with effectiveness to get them to even consider doing anything different."

"On the day of the team time trial, I probably didn't help either, because I was frustrated and trying to force the race and was then doing more harm than good. Greg was with me and could see what was going wrong in the training, but he didn't have the energy to get into the politics of it—and I was just the new guy, the quick new guy, but I couldn't really say anything. So there was just a terrible lack of communication. We all watched it unfold, probably knowing what was going to happen in that team time trial, and I think Greg could see that something needed to be done.

"Greg wasn't a big communicator then, but I think if it had been a few years earlier, it would have been a different story: he would have seen the problem. I do recall him doing a lot of organization, though . . . We started to ride longer turns, rather than going hard, because that was just killing everybody.

"The way that Greg revolutionized road cycling and changed the sport was through leadership. Because he was an innovator, he looked at the demands of the event, rather than the history. Greg was also in love with the sport, whereas I was in love with the challenge, but that probably swayed things. But when it came to the Tour, the team went for a three week race and I went for a seven minute race, so that was my preparation, my mindset, everything. Anything that came after those seven minutes was whatever it was.

"Greg and I had very different passions for the sport, but we had similar strategies and approaches that were different from the historical norm in professional cycling—where you'd ride your bike for forty hours a week and hope for the best. Which was nice, but it was just that the way we did it was more effective. Greg understood you needed to invest and prepare for specific things, and so did I. And I understood that aerodynamics were more important than anything else. We were embedded in a very traditional team who had no appetite for change, so we had to beat them over the head with effectiveness to get them to even consider doing anything different.

"[GAN] was my first professional team, and Roger Legeay was the first sports director I'd ever had, so I had no benchmark as to what he was or wasn't. I had this idea that they'd have all their strategies, and you'd be meeting them in a darkened room with a war board, and they'd be moving pieces around, sending these guys here and there . . . But the first time I met Legeay, I was amazed that he [was so open]. He asked me what I wanted to do, so I started telling him this and that, and his hand came up to stop me and he was smiling. He obviously thought I was being incredibly naive, but he went with it; he just wanted to write it all down on a piece of paper! I couldn't believe I was having so much say in what I wanted to do. I thought I'd just be a part of a bigger structure and have a role to play, so I don't know if it was old school or not. He was excited by new approaches and up for changing. Luckily, I demonstrated that it worked within six months.

"Eight years later, I fully appreciated what Greg was feeling in his last Tour. He still had the technical capability to do a good team time trial. He still had the experience to look after himself, measure his effort, and support the people around him, but the people around us were riding as individuals. They weren't bad or malicious, they just didn't know what [they were doing]. It's hard to know what's going on behind you, but they weren't thinking about the sprinters on the climbs. Regardless what anyone else was or wasn't doing [GAN eventually finished sixth on the team time trial stage], we just didn't get the best out of ourselves. It was embarrassing at that level that we didn't know and no one flagged it up.

"I remember riding the Dauphiné with Greg. I won the prologue by one second, and that was my last audition to get into the Tour de France. I remember during that race, he couldn't scratch himself [cycling slang for ride at full pace or hurt oneself]. There was nothing there, and he was clearly having difficult conversations with the management. It just wasn't going his way, but he was genuinely pleased for me, rather than feeling jealous. He constantly surprised me—his human generosity, such a nice man, genuinely interested in everything and everybody. At dinner, he would say, 'That was incredible, well done!' Which was amazing really, especially when he was having such a bad time of it. He'd said to me afterward, 'I'd be over the moon to win a prologue and I'm supposed to be winning this race.'

"I realize now that Greg was somebody who simply ran out of energy—not physical, but mental energy. He didn't believe it anymore; he didn't believe that it was possible."

"Greg revolutionized cycling because he could win. He forced a change in behavior. With salaries, he said, 'This is what an ordinary baseball player would be getting,' so he more or less doubled people's salaries. And the whole sunglasses endorsement thing—that was Greg. Aero helmets and triathlon bars . . . Okay, he wasn't the first person to do that, but because of that generosity of spirit, he wasn't precious about these ideas. He saw the power meter and wanted to use it. He adopted things and brought them together into cycling as a new package. I don't think he dug very deeply, though, because he didn't know what he didn't know, but he certainly raised the topic of aerodynamics with Boone Lennon's bars—and Greg's largely the person for popularizing those. He didn't dig very deeply into aerodynamics because one person can't do everything, but he knew there was something there. Greg was an innovator because he had the courage to be different.

"When I turned professional, in many ways it was a big step backwards technology-wise. Peter Keen and I had worked on the whole marginal gains concept. We worked with Lotus and had revelations about the importance of aerodynamics, and we had all that research. Professional cycling at that time was more like a cottage industry, where information changed from one team to another but nobody looked outside—so we went backwards in time. But that was brilliant for me because we got to steal a march on something, and that prologue in 1994 showed people what was possible.

"The big lesson was that if you bring someone into the sport who doesn't know the sport, they are more likely to change things and make big steps forward, because they don't know what they can't do. The Lotus frame was almost a misnomer—the primary importance of that era was the change in thinking. My position was so extreme, so low at the front. I had bars slammed right down; I was seven inches lower than even the most aero riders of the time. But there were riders who were just riding a bike straight out of Decathlon and were handed a pair of tri-bars but didn't really know what they were for. Greg could see it, just from looking at the bike, and he was fascinated when he saw me riding it. It didn't look wrong and I wasn't losing any power. He may well have been desperate to find something to help his form, but he had nothing to lose, because an innovator is also someone prepared to take a risk. And he had everything to gain.

"As far as his career was concerned, I realize now that he was somebody who simply ran out of energy—not physical, but mental energy. He didn't believe it anymore; he didn't believe that it was possible. And he was trying to work out how to finish it up. In the end, though, events overtook him. I remember when he climbed off at the Tour, they made him get back into the sag wagon, rather than one of the team cars. [The sag wagon is also known as the broom wagon, and usually has a broom attached to it. It's always the last vehicle in the race, and is used to pick up the stragglers. The fact that Greg had to go in it was a massive snub.] That was really poor treatment of this individual who'd done so much for the sport and probably got the team the sponsorship in the first place."

Tour de France
Greg and Chris both took equipment choice very seriously. Both thought it was worth the effort, and both proved it by becoming the fastest time trialists the Tour had ever seen.

93

Team: GAN

13th: Three Days of De Panne

25th: Tour of Flanders

53rd: Rund um den Henninger-Turm

Giro d'Italia (abandoned stage 20)

Tour de Romandie (abandoned)

Vuelta al País Vasco (abandoned)

94

Team: GAN

8th: First Union Grand Prix

11th: Three Days of De Panne

22nd: Tour DuPont
5th: prologue

28th: Classic Haribo

41st: Tour of Switzerland

42nd: Grand Prix E3 Harelbeke

47th: De Brabantse Pijl

140th: Milan–San Remo

Critérium du Dauphiné Libéré
3rd: stage 4 (race abandoned at a later stage)

Tour de France (abandoned stage 6)

1994 Tour de France
Race director Jean-Marie Leblanc talks to Greg during what would be his final Tour.

1993 Paris-Roubaix
In 1993, Greg's teammate Gilbert Duclos-Lassalle would win again. It's not just a hazardous race for the riders, the TV crews can also come unstuck.

gan

1994 Paris–Roubaix
"I'd had as much drive to win a classic as a Grand Tour."

Greg LeMond

1994 Tour de France: prologue
"Everybody says how hard a marathon is, yet twenty thousand people show up for New York. Only two hundred can enter the Tour de France, and it takes you years to get there. You can't just sign up for it."
Greg LeMond

1994 Tour de France: stage 6

"In the last seven years [of my career], I had four months when I felt good. And in those four months I won the Tour de France twice and the World Championships, but the rest of the time I was just struggling. I never needed to race and be the last guy, being pushed up hills, and that's who I was [in 1994]. And the last thing I wanted to be remembered as was the rider who stayed on too long. Now I'm retired, I'll try to have some fun."

Greg LeMond

1994 Tour de France: grand départ

"Cycling wasn't a brutal sport for me. For the average rider it was brutal, but not for me. I do think I was an exceptional talent. There's nothing more frustrating for an athlete than to be talented and then suddenly to have all that talent taken away from you."

Greg LeMond

GREG LEMOND
GREG LEMOND
GREG LEMOND

Bikes

"Stuff was brought to me because I was willing to try it."

GREG LEMOND

In less than ten years, Greg LeMond went from racing a relatively heavy ten-speed steel bike—set up as racing bikes had been for the previous fifty years—to a machine with essentially all the lightweight components and aerodynamic advances that are in use today. Throughout his career, Greg was adamant that it should be he who decided what equipment he was going to use, be it a Merlin titanium frame in team colors or an all-carbon Calfee frame complete with integrated brake and gear controls. In his last year as a professional, he even used Mavic Zap electronic shifting. And let's not forget the carbon wheels and clipless pedals that have remained relatively unchanged for two decades. So when Greg retired from racing, he was riding a bike not dissimilar to those that are ridden at the Tour de France today, some twenty years later.

Greg's willingness to try something different was another reason why he stood out from his peers. He refused to accept the usual team management policy of using only the sponsors' equipment. Indeed, even when his own fledgling bike brand sponsored his GAN team, he still looked elsewhere for the best frames and equipment he could find.

As well as spearheading the use of new technology, Greg was instrumental in shaping the explosion in branded racing and training accessories. He wasn't always the *first* to use them, but he was often the first *to be noticed* using them. And in some cases, that made all the difference to the commercial success—or otherwise—of a newly launched product: he was, in effect, a traveling salesman, helping to shift a lot of stock. Of the many products that were pioneered by Greg, most have had an influence on modern bike racing. The list is impressive: Avocet cycling computers; Grab-On racing handlebar covers; Look clipless pedals; full-length zippers for racing jerseys; Velcro straps for shoes; concealed brake cables; rear disc wheels; double disc wheels; 26 inch front wheels for time trial bikes; Cinelli Aero time trial helmets; Boone Lennon's Scott aero time trial handlebars (and, later, his Scott Drop-In road racing handlebars); Time pedals; index gear shifting; Campagnolo Ergopower brake and shift levers; gear shifters placed on the tri-bars; tri-spoked carbon time trial wheels; quad-spoked carbon time trial wheels; SRM power cranks and meters; various types of heart rate monitor; RockShox suspension forks for the Paris–Roubaix; Giro foam helmets; and Giro hard-shell helmets. And then, of course, there are the Oakley sunglasses: the Factory Pilot, the Blade, and the Razor Blade. He also developed a unique type of home trainer and a fitness brand: LeMond Fitness.

The following pages feature a selection of Greg's personal bike collection, photographed outside his house in Minnesota, on a small stretch of cobblestones he had built into his driveway. Needless to say, the cobbles are reclaimed porphyry cobbles brought over from France—the same as those used for the agricultural roads in the Nord and Pas de Calais regions of northern France over which countless riders in the Paris–Roubaix, Greg included, have ridden. Greg's collection of bikes ranges from "just raced" to totally renovated, but each has a story.

1990 Tour de France
Some technology never changes. Attaching tubular tires in the team Z truck.

1974
Cinelli Speciale Corsa

"I love it, it's gorgeous; the most beautiful bike I have. When I started, in '76, the bikes were either Raleighs or Italian, which were considered the real racing bikes at the time—usually Cinellis, because that's what we all thought the pros were using. So the only thing you had for racing bikes were Italian bikes: whatever came from Italy, that was the racing bike. My dad bought it, eight hundred bucks. We got it from Rick's Bike Shop in Reno, California; it'd been sitting there for two years. We bought it in 1976, and I ended up winning my first eleven races on it. That was the Cinelli, the only one in Reno. I remember that the guy at the bike shop didn't want to sell it to me. He said, 'It's too hard, kid. You'll never race.' Although I think he told everyone that! It had these steep angles, but it raced fine; it was a great bike. Okay, it was too big for me, but I raced with that in 1976 and through all of 1977.

"[Reno-based frame builder] Roland Della Santa was going to sponsor a team, so he built me a bike. I raced that for two years—forty, fifty races on it. A great bike. This Cinelli had a steeper head tube angle . . . but the Della Santa was a more traditional road racing bike. It was more relaxed, smaller, and more my size. Then, in 1979, a guy who owned a bike shop in Iowa sponsored me on a Raleigh, which I rode at the Junior World Championships; I was racing on a Raleigh, and I was also sponsored by Avocet. That bike was more traditional too. The top tube was shorter, which put you more 'over' the front wheel. But I started using the Cinelli in '77 or '78. I painted it on my second year, although I had it re-done in '89, back to its original state."

Greg LeMond

FRAME: Cinelli Speciale Corsa built with Columbus SL tubes
FORK: Cinelli sloping fork crown
HEADSET: Campagnolo
CRANKSET: Campagnolo Nuovo Record 42/52 and Record pedals, with Christophe clips and straps
GEAR LEVERS: Campagnolo Nuovo Record
FRONT DERAILLEUR: Campagnolo Nuovo Record
REAR DERAILLEUR: Campagnolo Nuovo Record
BRAKES: Campagnolo Nuovo Record
FREEWHEEL: Regina (with junior gears)
WHEELS: Campagonolo Nuovo Tipo Large Flange hubs on 32 hole Mavic rims
TIRES: Clement Criterium
SADDLE: Cinelli
SEATPOST: Campagnolo Nuovo Record
STEM: Cinelli 1A
HANDLEBARS: Cinelli 62—"Eddy Merckx"

ABOVE
1977: Nevada City
Still on the yellow bike, but he's ditched the yellow jersey—for now.

1983
Gitane Team Pro

"Most of the pros of the '80s and '90s were almost all riding racing production bikes, but the Gitane bikes were real racing bikes . . . Renault's bikes weren't mass-produced; they were handmade steel bikes, although it's possible that they weren't all custom-built. A steep, 73 degree head angle was typical on professionals' bikes, but we used very relaxed seat angles. The main reason they were doing this at the time was because the saddle and seatpost availability was limited, and therefore geometry choice was mostly for the position of the saddle. It's the wheelbase, head angle, and where the wheels are set that gives the bike its stability and comfort.

"I was using equipment in 1983 and 1984 that no one else was using. The aerodynamics were new as well. We used special low-profile time trial bikes, and nobody was paying attention to this apart from [Cyrille] Guimard. He'd already worked a lot with the Formula 1 wind tunnels. Also, Guimard did other groundbreaking studies on seat height and oxygen consumption, and his formula is what many people still use, even today. But the biggest change was that I was using heart rate monitors. I was sponsored by Avocet, which developed the handlebar mounted bike computer."

Greg LeMond

FRAME: Gitane Team Pro Issue—Columbus SL
FORK: Sloping crown
HEADSET: Stronglight A9 Alloy
CRANKSET: Stronglight 53/39
GEAR LEVERS: Simplex Retrofriction
FRONT DERAILLEUR: Simplex Prestige
REAR DERAILLEUR: Simplex Prestige SLJ 5500
BRAKES: Modolo Master Pro

FREEWHEEL: 6 speed Maillard
WHEELS: Maillard hubs, 32 hole Mavic SSC rims
TIRES: Vittoria CX Servizio Corse
SADDLE: Selle Italia Turbo
SEATPOST: Cinelli 1R
STEM: Cinelli 1A
HANDLEBARS: Cinelli 62—"Eddy Merckx"

OPPOSITE
1983 Critérium du Dauphiné Libéré
Greg is led by Marc Madiot. Both men were riding for a French team on a fully French-equipped bike.

1986
La Vie Claire Team Reynolds 753

In 1986, all professional teams had a bicycle sizing chart. They still do. This chart tells the mechanics the riders' frame sizes, seat height, their preferred saddle position, handlebar height, and angle of the brake levers—all in minute detail—so that whatever bike the rider picks up with his name on it, it will fit him immediately. The team's bike sponsors also have this information relayed to them, even receiving the riders' preferences over materials.

In the steel-frame era, and depending on the factory's capability, these bikes would be built each winter in preparation for the coming spring and the start of the racing season. Brands that didn't have a frame workshop sent the work out to small contractors. Often, these would be individuals or family-run businesses producing custom-built steel frames, rather than the mass-produced factory standards.

For most of the twentieth century, the professional peloton was dominated by Italian brands, so most frames came from Italian contractors—even when the bike brand was based elsewhere. Professional riders would even choose their own bike builder, somebody nearby who they trusted and had a close association with. The bikes were then provided raw and unpainted to the sponsor's factory, where they were sprayed with the team livery. American riders were no different: Andy Hampsten rode a Serotta, Greg LeMond a Della Santa. In the United Kingdom, Sean Yates would ride a Cliff Shrubb, and Dave Akam a Ron Cooper. This subcontractor arrangement is the likely source of the Hinault-branded bikes La Vie Claire rode in the 1985 and 1986 seasons. Light, strong, and responsive, they were built from Reynolds 753 tubing—the finest on offer at the time.

FRAME: Hinault-La Vie Claire Team edition Reynolds 753
FORK: 753 unicrown
HEADSET: Campagnolo C-Record
CRANKSET: Campagnolo C-Record
GEAR LEVERS: Campagnolo Super Record
FRONT DERAILLEUR: Campagnolo C-Record
REAR DERAILLEUR: Campagnolo Super Record
BRAKES: Campagnolo Super Record with C-Record levers and concealed cables
FREEWHEEL: 7 speed Sachs
WHEELS: Campagnolo C-Record hubs on Mavic rims
TIRES: Michelin
SADDLE: Selle San Marco Rolls
SEATPOST: Campagnolo C-Record
STEM: Cinelli 1R
HANDLEBARS: Cinelli 62—"Eddy Merckx"

OPPOSITE, BOTTOM
Tour de France: stage 20
Greg pushes a huge gear, uphill, on his way to winning the '86 Tour.

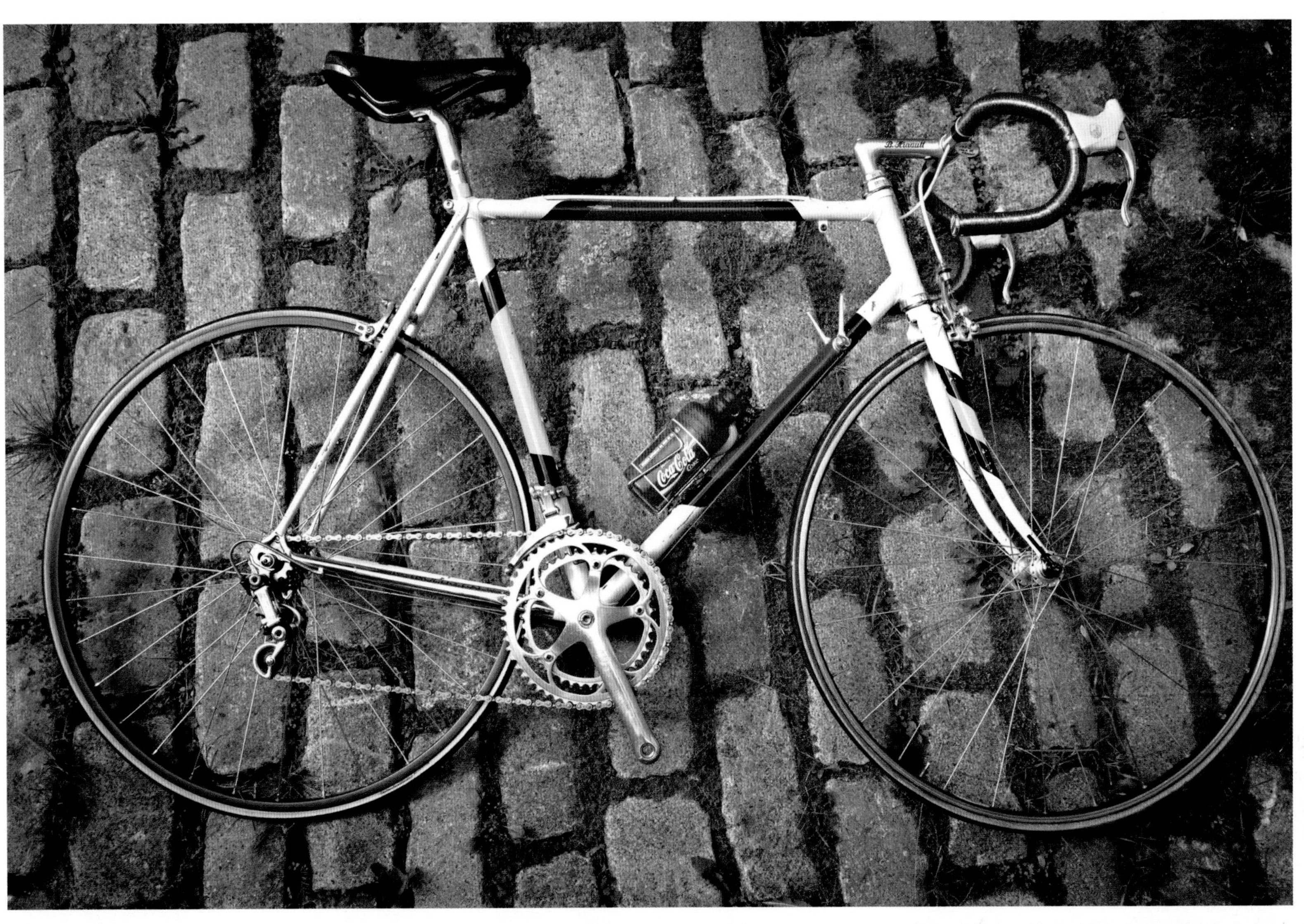
Coca-Cola

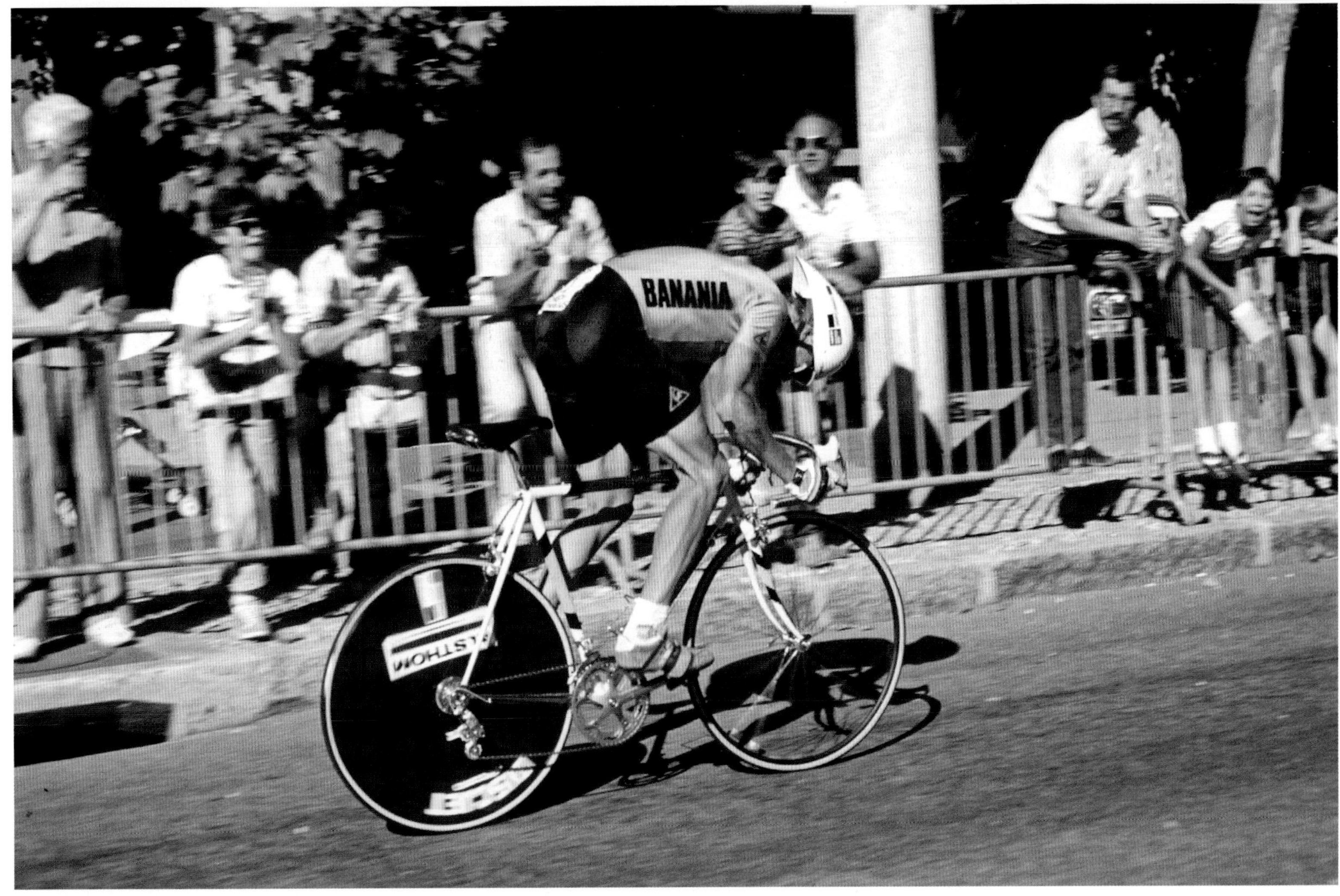
BANANIA

1989
Bottecchia Time Trial

"That Bottecchia is really heavy, but was actually pretty aero."
Greg LeMond

This bike was built in Italy, no doubt by a frame-building contractor, since Bottecchia had most of its bikes made out of house. The seatpost is from the Columbus Air tubing set. The seat tube had an aero section, rather than being completely round, so it needed a specially made seatpost fitting. Because Greg used it for the 1990 season, the bike is shown here (opposite, top) in the colors of team Z.

The smaller, 26 inch front wheel lowered the height of the front of the bike considerably, and thus the frontal area of the bike and rider. Very often, however, this resulted in the rider becoming very straight-armed and uncomfortable, if not using triathlon bars. It also meant that the bike wasn't the easiest to control around corners.

Greg's use of triathlon handlebars (or tri-bars) caused some controversy, with some of the team officials kicking up a fuss. Some even argued that they were unsafe. Fignon tried the bars before the closing time trial stage of the '89 Tour, but decided not to use them. All the decisions on equipment went Greg's way that day: with a strong wind blowing, he decided to use a spoked front wheel rather than the double disc wheels Fignon used, which could catch the crosswinds and make the bike unpredictable to steer and harder to handle at speed when cornering.

The judges deemed Greg's use of the tri-bars to be fair, and from that point on, everyone used them in time trials—especially Laurent Fignon. This beautifully made but heavy steel bike became one of the fastest and most valuable in Tour de France history.

FRAME: Bottecchia Crono built from Columbus Air tubing
FORK: 26 inch Columbus Air
HEADSET: Campagnolo C-Record
CRANKSET: Mavic 631 "Starfish" 54/46
GEAR LEVERS: Mavic Retrofriction (on ADR original)
FRONT DERAILLEUR: Mavic 840
REAR DERAILLEUR: Mavic 840
BRAKES: Mavic 651 (Mavic SSC on ADR original)
FREEWHEEL: Compact time trial ratios

WHEELS: Campagnolo hub with Mavic Mach 2 CD SSC rim and bladed aero spokes front wheel; Mavic Comete Carbone Disc rear wheel
TIRES: Vittoria
SADDLE: Selle Italia Turbomatic Fausto Coppi (on ADR original)
SEATPOST: Columbus Air
STEM: Mavic
HANDLEBARS: Mavic TT cow horns with Scott Aero tri-bars

ABOVE **1989 Tour de France**
Greg didn't need time checks. He kept it simple and just went faster.

OPPOSITE, BOTTOM
1989 Tour de France: stage 5
Judges examine the Scott tri-bars ahead of the Dinard time trial.

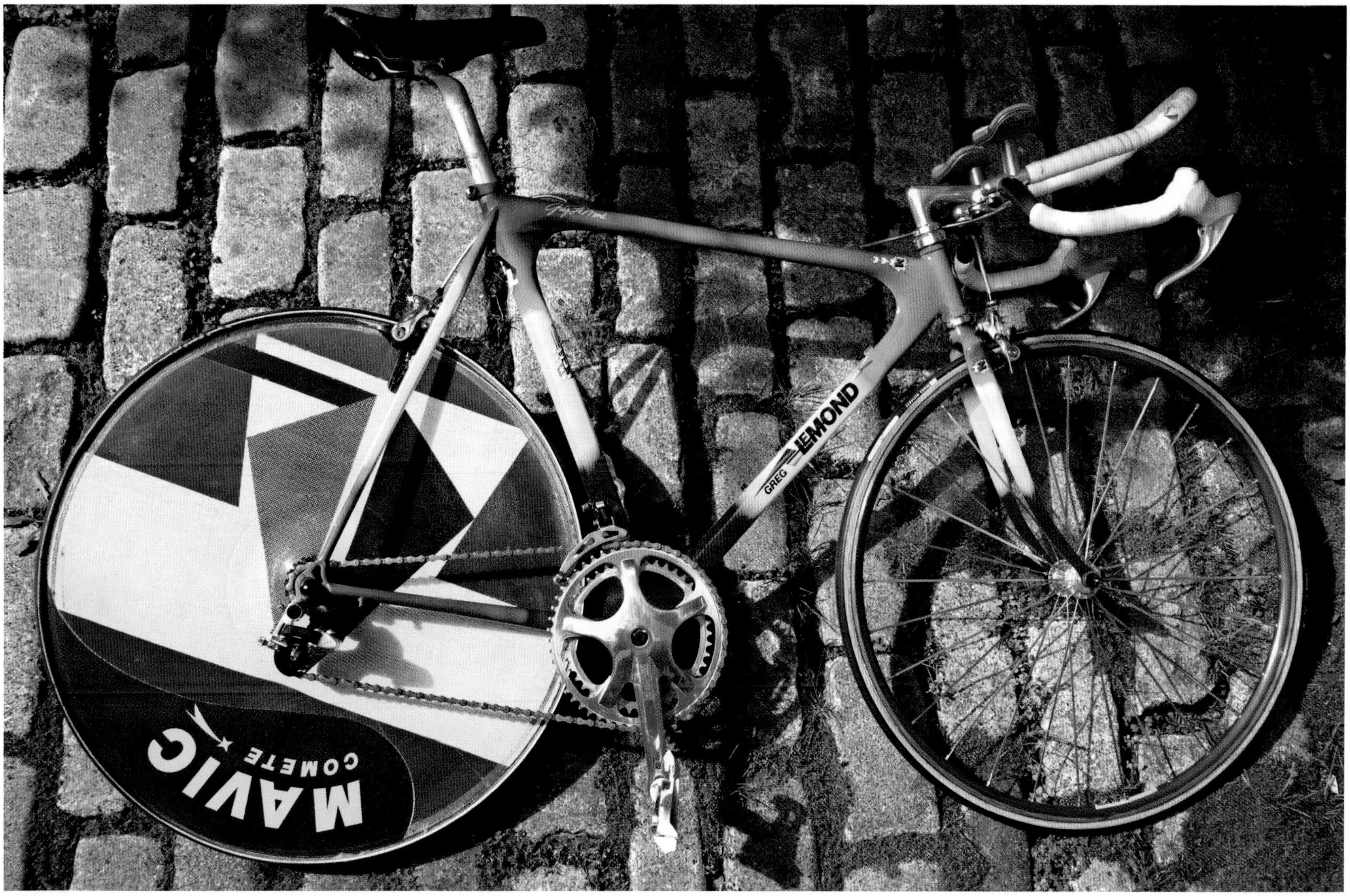

GREG LEMOND
MAVIC
COMETE

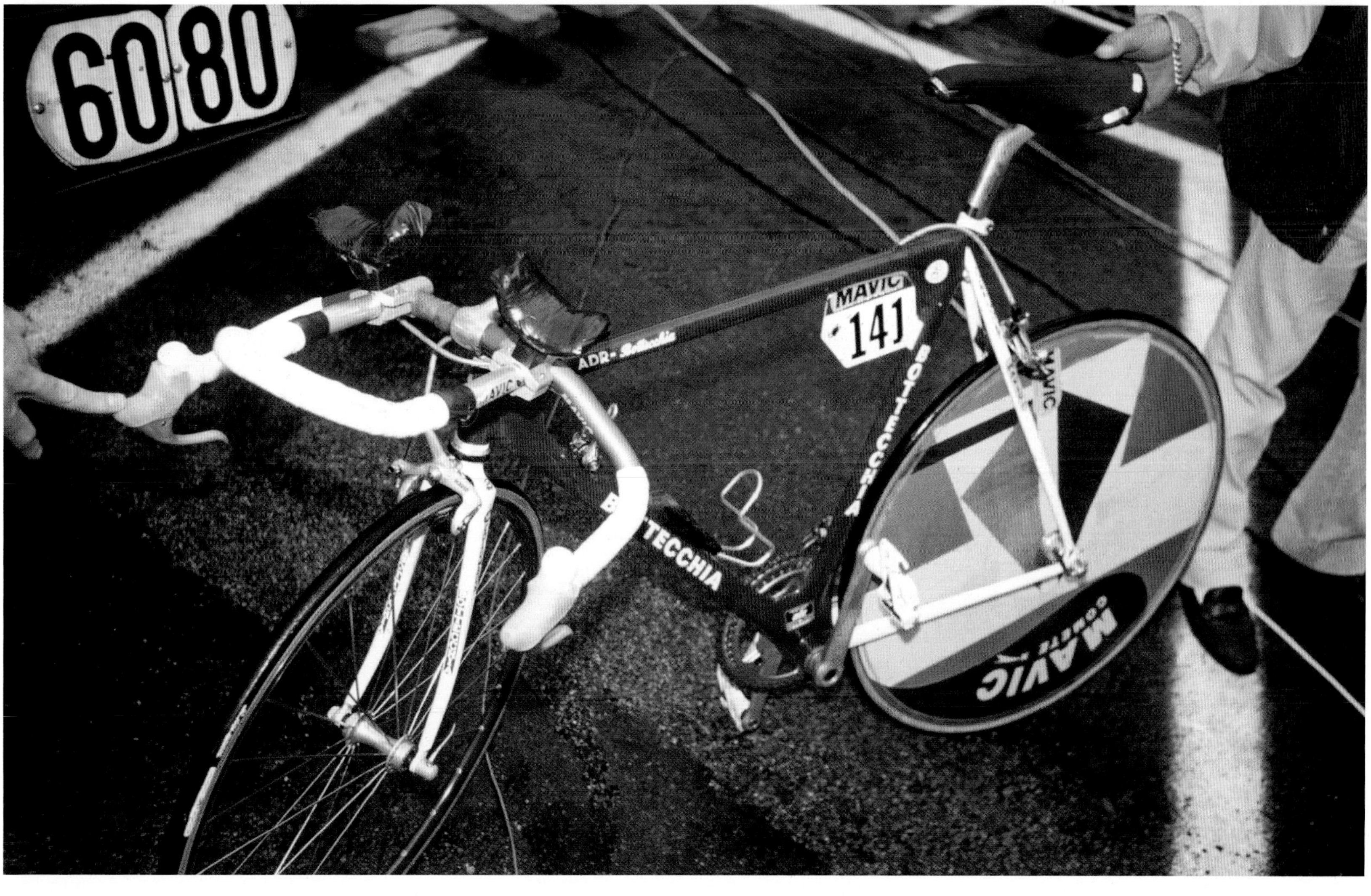

60 80
MAVIC
141
ADR
BOTTECCHIA
MAVIC
COMETE

1989

RIGHT **1989 Tour de France** The mountain time trial on stage 15.

"My favorite bikes, from a riding perspective, are steel bikes. But I really liked the carbon TVT [bike]. I used that for the Tour and for the Worlds. TVT was the company that made the tubes, and the engineer Jean-Marc Gueugneaud had developed the process of the bonding or adhesion of aluminum lugs to the carbon fiber tubes. After leaving the Look pedal company, Jean-Marc launched TVT, a custom carbon fiber manufacturer, which provided production bikes for riders like myself, Pedro Delgado, and Miguel Indurain. I won three Tours and one World Championships on a TVT."

Greg LeMond

FRAME: TVT 92 Carbone ADR "Maillot Jaune"
FORK: TVT carbon bladed fork
HEADSET: Mavic
CRANKSET: Mavic 631 "Starfish"
GEAR LEVERS: Campagnolo C-Record
FRONT DERAILLEUR: Mavic 851 SSC
REAR DERAILLEUR: Mavic 851 SSC
BRAKES: Mavic Speedy
FREEWHEEL: Mavic
WHEELS: Mavic 851 hubs on Mavic Mach 2 CD rims
TIRES: Vittoria CX
SADDLE: Selle San Marco Rolls
SEATPOST: Stronglight
STEM: Mavic SSC
HANDLEBARS: Cinelli 62—"Eddy Merckx"

1990

RIGHT **1990 Tour de France**
Greg on a TVT at the Z team presentation before the départ.

"Jean-Marc Gueugneaud came to La Vie Claire in February 1986 to convince me and Hinault to use his new bikes, so we used them in the Tour. I loved the ride: it was safe and probably a kilo lighter than a steel team bike. In 1988, he built a bike in case I did the Tour de France. He kept building bikes for me in case I came back. He had this fluorescent one built in ADR colors [opposite, top] in 1989. I wanted the freedom to ride anything without the influence of a sponsor. I wanted the flexibility and to able to use the best equipment, which is why I started my bike company in 1986. The only advancements in today's bikes are the quality of carbon fiber and the weight."

Greg LeMond

FRAME: TVT Carbone 92 Team Z
FORK: TVT
HEADSET: Campagnolo C-Record
CRANKSET: Campagnolo Record 53/39
GEAR LEVERS: Campagnolo 8 speed Syncro 2
FRONT DERAILLEUR: Campagnolo Record
REAR DERAILLEUR: Campagnolo Record
BRAKES: Campagnolo Delta Record
FREEWHEEL: Campagnolo
WHEELS: Campagnolo Record 8 speed hubs
TIRES: Vittoria Corsa CG Squadra Pro
SADDLE: Selle San Marco Regal
SEATPOST: Campagnolo C-Record
STEM: 3-TTT Record
HANDLEBARS: Scott Drop-In Bar

1992
Calfee all-carbon

"I wished for some feedback for improving the bike, but Greg said it was perfect—unless there was a way to make it even lighter. Greg relied on experts and was willing to take risks and try them out. That innovation and constant improvement are welcomed at the highest level—at least so long as the top rider is sponsoring the bikes. But Greg explained it to me fairly well when he said, 'Let's say I'm riding a bike that's heavier than Indurain's bike. Assuming that we're in the same condition and we're climbing Alpe d'Huez, if Indurain is on a lighter bike and I know this, I'm going to give up. I won't push myself as hard. I need to have the best bike.'

"JP Pascal [from the Time pedal company] was very supportive of what we were doing. He and Greg saw that the future was made of carbon fiber, and we had customers who were willing to try it. However, many of the team riders were skeptical. Greg's big Dutch domestique, Johan Lammerts, said that he'd destroy it—but he couldn't. The old man of the Z team, Gilbert Duclos-Lassalle, liked how light the bike was, although he didn't like the space between the down tube and the front tire, so he had me cut the bottom of the head tube to make a smaller space there. It had the effect of steepening the head and seat tube angles almost half a degree, but he liked the quick handling. But the bike's ride quality, stiffness, and strength, and the fact we can do custom geometry, made it exactly what Greg was looking for—so I think we nailed it. Nowadays, the pro teams don't get custom frames any more; they get what the bike company sponsors want to sell. But I just stick with what makes a better bike.

"With Greg, we had the rare circumstance where the driving force of the bike sponsor was winning the race, rather than any other business objective—although Greg riding our bike was undoubtedly our big break. His continued support and friendship means a lot to me, and he knows I am always here to help with whatever I can. Looking back, I can also say I have been inspired by his determination and steadfast integrity. And that may be the thing that lasts the longest."

Craig Calfee

FRAME: Calfee
FORK: Calfee
HEADSET: Mavic sealed roller bearing
CRANKSET: Mavic 631 "Starfish" 53/39
GEAR LEVERS: Campagnolo Record Ergopower 8 speed (Mavic Zap on 1994 time trial bike)
FRONT DERAILLEUR: Campagnolo Record
REAR DERAILLEUR: Campagnolo Record

BRAKES: Campagnolo Record Delta
FREEWHEEL: Campagnolo
WHEELS: Campagnolo Record rear hub, Mavic GP4 rims
TIRES: Vittoria CX
SADDLE: Selle San Marco 650 Karbonio
SEATPOST: Campagnolo C-Record
STEM: Cinelli Grammo Titanium
HANDLEBARS: Mavic

OPPOSITE, BOTTOM
1992 Tour de France: stage 9
Greg rode his Calfee road bike, with aerodynamic additions, to fifth place in the Luxembourg time trial.

1986 Tour de France
Greg LeMond: yellow jersey racer.

Acknowledgments

First and foremost, I'd like to thank the LeMond family—Kathy, Greg, Simone, Geoff, and Scott—for allowing me into their home and putting up with me rummaging around in their basement. I couldn't have made this book without their help and blessing. I'd also like to thank Ian Slingsby, Rob Rees, Viv McDonald, and Joe, Vic, and Simon Marshall, my fellow travelers on my journey to France in 1986 to witness my first Tour. That trip has much to do with why I decided to put this book together, instilling in me a deep passion for the sport of bike racing, one that's never left me. Thank you, all.

My heartfelt thanks and appreciation also go to every one of Greg's friends, rivals, and teammates who gave up their time to be interviewed for this book. Special thanks go to those who helped me line up those interviews, including Harry Maidment from Eurosport, Christelle Tanguy from Ronan Pensec Travel, Christel Roche from Stephen Roche Travel, Alex Jacome, and Ned Boulting.

Thanks to the design team of Pete Dawson and Namkwan Cho at Grade Design in London. Then there are all the friends and colleagues with whom I discussed the project or who contributed to the process. Many have had to put up with me banging on about it on bike rides or during phone calls, but their help, friendship, and loyalty is much appreciated. They are Jay Barbour, Cathal MacIlwaine, Mark Beisiegel, Rufus Olins, David Pearl, Nadav Kander, Colin O'Brien, Craig Calfee, Matt Seaton, David Millar, Robert Millar, Kevin Fitzpatrick, Brian Palmer, James and Louise Cavanagh, Zoe Wassall, Dan Marsh, Rohan Dubash, Kadir Guirey, Jim Andrews, James Startt, Sarah Skipper, Jeremy Dunn, Kim Ritchey, Gino, and underdogs everywhere. Also, my thanks to the editorial help and attention to detail of Mark Ralph and Colm McAuliffe.

There are numerous people to thank at the archives we used for this project, especially at *L'Equipe*, and many thanks go to Olivier Michon and Fabrice Leboulanger, whose patience as we trawled the extensive archives in Paris was admirable. Thanks, as well, to Mark Leech and Charlotte Wilson from Offside in London for helping set that up. I'd especially like to thank the *L'Equipe* photographers who worked on the cycle racing circuit in Greg's days: Denis Clément, Patrick Boutroux, Jean-Claude Pichon, Bernard Papon, and Michel Deschamps. Their work is inspirational and exceptional, in both quality and resonance. At Getty Images, thanks are due to Toby Hopkins and photographers Pascal Pavani, Graham Finlayson, and Pascal Rondeau. And finally, my thanks to the individual photographers who also contributed work: Phil O'Connor, Beth Schneider, Cor and Carla Vos, and John Pierce. On the picture editing and production side, my very special thanks to Taz Darling, Eoin Houllihan, Eric Ladd, and Linda Duong.

Lastly, a huge thank you to our publishing partners: Ted Costantino and Casey Blaine at VeloPress, Charlotte Croft at Bloomsbury, and Simon Mottram and Daniel Blumire at Rapha, all of whom believed in the project and helped us to realize it.

Picture Credits

© Offside/l'Equipe
Front cover, 1, 7, 8, 11, 13, 31, 41, 42b, 44, 45, 46, 47, 48, 50, 52, 55, 56, 57, 59, 60, 61, 62, 64, 66, 74, 76, 77, 78, 79, 83, 84, 85, 86b, 87, 96, 97, 98, 99, 101, 102, 103, 105, 107, 108, 110, 111, 112, 114, 116, 119, 120, 122, 123, 125, 126, 127, 128, 130, 131, 132, 133, 134, 135, 136, 137, 138, 139, 141, 142, 142, 143, 144, 151, 152, 154, 155, 156, 157, 158, 159, 160t, 161, 162, 164, 165, 166, 168, 169, 170, 171, 172, 173, 174, 181, 182l, 184, 186, 192, 195, 196, 197, 200, 202, 208, 209, 210, 211, 212, 213, 214, 215, 218, 219, 220, 222, 224, 228, 230, 231, 232, 233, 234, 235, 236, 241, 243, 244, 246, 247, 248, 255, 257, 259, 260, 261, 262, 263b, 266t, 267, 269, 271, 272, 280, 281, 282, 283, 287, 288, 293b, 295b, 296, 297b, 298b, 299b, 301b, 302

© Cor Vos Images
68, 71, 88, 92, 106, 160b, 188, 193, 223, 242, 250, 258, 270, 274, 284, 285

© Photosport International
63, 82, 129, 146, 182r, 199, 205, 239, 245, 264

© Beth Schneider
20, 90, 95, 121, 153, 175, 194, 198, 206, 226, 237, 252, 266b

© Greg LeMond
15, 18, 22, 24, 25, 26, 27, 28, 29, 30, 32, 34, 36, 39, 40, 42t, 43, 72, 86t, 176, 221, 256, 263t, 290, 304

© Guy Andrews
291, 292, 293t, 294, 295t, 297t, 298t, 299t, 300, 301t

© Phil O'Connor
4, 279

© Getty Images
16, 73, 80, 81, 216, 276, 286

1982 Tour de l'Avenir: stage 10
With the Colombian Israel Fonseca on the way to Morzine.